# Positive Youth Development Through Sport

Young people are too frequently looked upon as problems waiting to be solved. From the perspective of Positive Youth Development (PYD), however, young people are understood to embody potential, awaiting development.

Sport provides a developmental context that has been associated with PYD, but sport by itself does not lead to PYD. In some environments negative outcomes can also arise from sport participation. It is the manner in which sport is structured and delivered to children that influences their development. The aim of this book is to explore research and practice relating to the structure and delivery of youth sport in order to shed further light on its use as a developmental context to promote PYD.

*Positive Youth Development Through Sport* fills a void in the literature by bringing together experts from diverse disciplines to critically examine the ways in which sport can be and has been used.

**Nicholas L. Holt** is an Associate Professor in the Faculty of Physical Education and Recreation at the University of Alberta, Canada.

## International studies in physical education and youth sport
Series editor: Richard Bailey
Roehampton University, London, UK

Routledge's International Studies in Physical Education and Youth Sport series aims to stimulate discussion on the theory and practice of school physical education, youth sport, childhood physical activity and well-being. By drawing on international perspectives, both in terms of the background of the contributors and the selection of the subject matter, the series seeks to make a distinctive contribution to our understanding of issues that continue to attract attention from policy-makers, academics and practitioners.

**Also available in this series:**

# Positive Youth Development Through Sport

Edited by Nicholas L. Holt

Routledge
Taylor & Francis Group

LONDON AND NEW YORK

First published 2008
by Routledge
2 Park Square, Milton Park, Abingdon, Oxon OX14 4RN

Simultaneously published in the USA and Canada
by Routledge
270 Madison Ave, New York, NY 10016

*Routledge is an imprint of the Taylor & Francis Group, an informa business*

© 2008 selection and editorial matter, Nicholas L. Holt; individual
chapters, the contributors

Typeset in Goudy by
HWA Text and Data Management, Tunbridge Wells
Printed and bound in Great Britain by
TJI Digital, Padstow, Cornwall

*British Library Cataloguing in Publication Data*
A catalogue record for this book is available from the British Library

*Library of Congress Cataloging-in-Publication Data*
Positive youth development through sport / [edited by] Nicholas L. Holt.
 p.  cm.
 1. Sports for children. 2. Sports for children–Social aspects. 3. Physical
 education for children. 4. Physical fitness for youth. I. Holt, Nicholas L.
GV709.2.P68 2007
796.083–dc22                                          2007004352

ISBN10: 0–415–77152–8 (hbk)
ISBN10: 0–203–94478–X (ebk)

ISBN13: 978–0–415–77152–8 (hbk)
ISBN13: 978–0–203–94478–3 (ebk)

# Contents

# Figures and tables

## Figures

## Tables

# Contributors

**Andy Anderson** is an Associate Professor at the Ontario Institute for Studies in Education at the University of Toronto. His research and development work include the role of health-promoting schools in developing countries and the development of health literacy.

**Kathleen M. Armour** is a Reader in Physical Education and Sport Pedagogy in the School of Sport and Exercise Sciences, Loughborough University, UK. Her main research interests are career-long professional learning for teachers and coaches, and its impact on young people's learning in physical education and sport.

**Richard Bailey** is Professor of Pedagogy at Froebel College, Roehampton University, where he works in the areas of philosophy of education and physical education. He was the director of the influential Sport in Education project, which was funded by the IOC, and involved fieldwork in every continent of the world, and was the rapporteur of the Physical Education and Sport section of UNESCO's 2004 Athens Declaration.

**Jennifer Carrano** is a doctoral student in Applied Development and Educational Psychology at Boston College and a research assistant at the Institute for Applied Research in Youth Development at Tufts University. Her research interests include positive youth development and public policy.

**John Corlett** is a Professor and Dean of Applied Health Sciences at Brock University. He has published book chapters and refereed journal articles on child growth in developing countries, on international education, on the role of sport in African nations, and on the role of physical education in achieving national development goals.

**Allen Cornelius** is a Research Scientist at Springfield College, MA, where he is Commissioner of Research for the National Football Foundation Center for Youth Development through Sport. He conducts research on youth development through sport and specializes in program evaluation.

**Jean Côté** is an Associate Professor and acting Director of the School of Kinesiology and Health Studies at Queen's University at Kingston, Ontario,

Canada. His research interests are in the areas of children in sport, positive youth development, and coaching.

**Steven Danish** is Director of the Life Skills Center and Professor of Psychology, Preventive Medicine and Community Health at Virginia Commonwealth University. Dr Danish is a licensed psychologist as well as a registered sport psychologist and conducts research on sports programs.

**Rebecca Duncombe** is a Research Associate within the Institute of Youth Sport at Loughborough University, UK. Her research interests include continuing professional development for physical education teachers and sport as a vehicle for re-engaging disaffected youth.

**Kristen Fay** is a MA/PhD student in the Eliot-Pearson Department of Child Development, Tufts University and a Graduate Research Assistant on the 4-H Study of Positive Youth Development. Kristen also collaborates with Dr Anne Becker at Massachusetts General Hospital in Boston. Her research interests include personal and contextual correlates of youth eating and weight disorders.

**Tanya Forneris** is an Assistant Professor in the School of Kinesiology and Health Studies at Queen's University at Kingston, Ontario, Canada. The primary focus of her research is developing, implementing and evaluating physical activity and sport-based life skills programming for youth.

**Jessica Fraser-Thomas** is a Post-Doctoral Fellow in the School of Kinesiology and Health Studies at Queen's University at Kingston, Ontario, Canada. Her research focuses on children and adolescents in sport in the areas of sport dropout and positive youth development.

**Ihirangi Heke** is an elite athlete mental skills trainer, and Lecturer in Physical Education at the University of Otago, New Zealand. He has also had involvement as both a player and coach in several sports. His most recent research has been in the area of life skills development with indigenous peoples.

**Don Hellison** is Professor of Education and Co-Director of the Responsible Youth Through Sport Program. His work focuses on urban youth development through physical activity.

**Ken Hodge** is an Associate Professor in sport and exercise psychology at the School of Physical Education, University of Otago, New Zealand. His research focuses on the psycho-social effects of participation in sport. He is currently an Associate Editor for the *Journal of Applied Sport Psychology*.

**Nicholas L. Holt** is an Associate Professor in the Faculty of Physical Education and Recreation at the University of Alberta, and the director of the Child and Adolescent Sport and Activity lab. He conducts research on youth sport and positive youth development.

**Martin I. Jones** is a doctoral student in the School of Sport and Exercise Sciences at Loughborough University, UK. He has research interests in youth sport, positive youth development, and athlete career education. Martin is a former county junior tennis player and currently coaches junior tennis.

**Richard M. Lerner** is the Bergstrom Chair in Applied Development Science in the Eliot-Pearson Department of Child Development, and the Director of the Institute for Applied Research in Youth Development, at Tufts University. His scholarship integrates the study of public policies and community-based programs with the promotion of positive youth development and youth contributions to civil society.

**Yibing Li** is a MA/PhD student in the Eliot-Pearson Department of Child Development at Tufts University, and a research assistant in the Institute for Applied Research in Youth Development. She is interested in the schooling and out-of-school time of youth.

**James Mandigo** is an Associate Professor in the Department of Physical Education and Kinesiology and Co-Director for the Centre for Healthy Development through Sport and Physical Activity at Brock University. His research and development work involve ways in which physical education is a vehicle towards the healthy development of individuals, their communities, and their countries.

**Tom Martinek** is a Professor in the Department of Exercise and Sport Science at the University of North Carolina at Greensboro. He coordinates the Community Youth Sport Development undergraduate program as well as teaches in several after-school youth sport programs with his students.

**Jack S. Peltz** is a graduate Research Assistant at Tufts University's Institute for Applied Research in Youth Development. He is currently working at the 4-H Study of Positive Youth Development.

**Albert J. Petitpas** is a Professor in the Psychology Department and Director of the National Football Foundation Center for Youth Development through Sport at Springfield College. He has provided consulting services to a wide range of sport organizations including The First Tee, the NCAA, NBA, NFL, USOC, US Ski Team, Play It Smart, and the LPGA.

**Rachel A. Sandford** is a Research Associate with the Institute of Youth Sport at Loughborough University, UK. Her research interests include issues relating to young people, embodied identity, and popular physical culture. She is currently evaluating the impact of physical activity programs designed to promote positive youth development through outdoor physical activity.

**Zoë L. Sehn** is an MA student in the Faculty of Physical Education and Recreation at the University of Alberta and is conducting research on the influence of sport and physical activity on positive youth development for inner-city youth.

**Leisha Strachan** is a doctoral student in the School of Kinesiology and Health Studies at Queen's University at Kingston, Ontario, Canada. Her research interests include topics relating to elite youth athletes, positive youth development, and using an ecological approach to examining youth in sport.

**Christina Theokas** is a development psychologist who works for Alexandria City Public Schools and has an adjunct faculty position at Virginia Commonwealth University. She conducts research on the role of the ecology (families, schools, neighborhoods, and after-school programs) on youth development.

**Judy Van Raalte** is Professor of Psychology and Director of the Athletic Counseling master's program at Springfield College in Springfield, Massachusetts. Her research interests include self-talk and sport performance, professional issues in sport psychology, body issues, and sport injury. She served as coach of the women's tennis team for five years, is co-editor of the text, *Exploring Sport and Exercise Psychology*, and is executive producer of 13 sport psychology videos.

**Dave Walsh** is in the Department of Kinesiology at San Francisco State University, where he directs the Urban Youth Development Project and supervises physical activity programs for underserved youth in San Francisco.

**Nicole Zarrett** is a Post-Doctoral Fellow at the Institute for Applied Research in Youth Development, Tufts University. Her research focuses on identifying differences in how youth spend their out-of-school time by environmental, familial and person-related factors to determine how youth, nested within their families and neighborhoods, and activities operate together to promote positive development.

# Acknowledgements

I would like to thank each of the contributors who have helped to create this volume. My special thanks is extended to Professor Richard Bailey, who invited me to edit this volume as part of his series of International Perspectives on Physical Education and Sport. I would also like to acknowledge my graduate students, administrative, and faculty colleagues at the University of Alberta for their support, particularly Dr John Spence, who has been a sounding board for my half-baked ideas for several years.

During the preparation of this volume I was fortunate to be supported by several sources of funding. My Population Health Investigator Award from the Alberta Heritage Foundation for Medical Research has enabled me to devote the majority of my time to research endeavors. I have also been supported by operating grants from the Social Sciences and Humanities Research Council, Canadian Institutes of Health Research, Centre for Urban Health Initiatives, Alberta Centre for Child, Family, and Community Research, and the Sport Science Association of Alberta. All of these sources of funding are greatly appreciated.

Finally, thanks to my friends outside academia (especially Mick and Cristian), and my family (Carole, Josie, Juno, and Alis), all of whom help to keep me relatively sane.

Nicholas L. Holt
December 2006
Edmonton, Alberta, Canada

# Abbreviations

| | |
|---|---|
| ASDAN | Award Scheme Development and Accreditation Network |
| DMSP | Developmental Model of Sport Participation |
| GOAL | Going for Goal |
| LfS | Living for Sport |
| NFFC@SC | National Football Foundation Center for Youth Development at Springfield College |
| OB | Outward Bound |
| OST | Out-of-school time |
| PACE | Promoting Academic Coach Excellence |
| PE | Physical Education |
| PYD | Positive Youth Development |
| PPCT | Person-Process-Context-Time |
| PQA | Program Quality Assessment |
| QPE | Quality Physical Education |
| RAP | Rugby Advantage Program |
| SUPER | Sports United to Promote Education and Recreation |
| TFT | The First Tee |
| TPRS | Teaching Personal and Social Responsibility |
| UIC | University of Illinois at Chicago |
| UNCG | University of North Carolina at Greensboro |
| UK | United Kingdom |
| UN | United Nations |
| US | United States |
| YST | Youth Sport Trust |
| YES | Youth Experience Survey |
| ZONE | Zeroing in On Network Excellence |

# Introduction: positive youth development through sport

*Nicholas L. Holt*

## The New View of Youth Development

This book primarily deals with the adolescent period of development. Adolescence is regarded as a period of transitions between childhood and adulthood, and may be broadly divided into three phases; early (11–14 years), middle (15–18 years) and late (19–21 years) (Steinberg 1993). Adolescents must deal with a range of biological, social, emotional, and psychological transitions in order to successfully enter the adult world (Coleman and Roker, 1998). Historically, adolescence was regarded as a period of 'sturm und drang' (storm and stress). Hall (1904) suggested that it was normal for adolescents to alternate between extremes of sorrow and exuberance, and shift unexpectedly between friendly altruism and selfish hoarding. However, adolescent storm and stress may have been given disproportionate emphasis by studying individuals already in turmoil (Offer 1969). Researchers came to recognize the need to examine both negative and positive aspects of the transitions adolescents encounter (Coles 1995). Whereas certain individuals may have heightened sensitivity to change during adolescence, others may have sufficient personal resources to successfully cope with the transitions they face in order to make a healthy and successful entry into adulthood (Graber and Brooks-Gunn 1997).

The tendency to view adolescence as a time of storm and stress was associated with a deficit-reduction approach, whereby researchers examined ways to prevent and/or reduce the problems adolescents may encounter. Over the past 15 years a new vision of adolescent development has emerged; this vision has been labeled positive youth development (PYD). Proponents of positive development (e.g. Benson 2003; Catalano *et al.* 1999; Damon 2004; Eccles and Gootman 2002) generally view all young people as having the potential for positive developmental change, and regard youth as a resource to be developed rather than a problem to be solved (Roth *et al.* 1998). Thus, PYD represents a strength-based conception of development rather than a deficit-reduction approach (Lerner *et al.* 2005).

Although PYD is the term used to describe this vision for positive adolescent development, it has no singular definition. The 'newness' of this field is reflected by the fact that the term PYD has yet to be fully embraced in the literature. King *et al.* (2005) reviewed the adolescent development literature from 1991 to 2003 to examine the terminology used to describe concepts consistent with PYD. Although 16 different terms were identified, five (competence, coping, health, resilience, and well-being) were most popular. This led King *et al.* to conclude that 'a rich nomological network of concepts pertinent to PYD has yet to emerge in the research literature of adolescent development' (p. 226). In the knowledge that there is no widely accepted definition of PYD, but in attempt to help define the focus of this book a little more clearly, I have adopted a definition of 'positive development' from Roth *et al.* (1998). They suggested that 'positive development is defined as the engagement in prosocial behaviors and avoidance of health compromising behaviors and future jeopardizing behaviors' (p. 426). This definition of positive development is broad enough to include a variety of PYD research perspectives. Indeed, the present volume is intended to provide a range of perspectives on ways in which PYD can be fostered through sporting activities.

## Positive Youth Development and Sport

Organized activities can provide youth with opportunities to experience PYD (Larson 2000). Sport is the most popular organized activity in which youth engage (Larson and Verma 1999). Therefore, the objective of this book is to explore ways in which sport may promote PYD. Given that this book is part of a series titled 'International Perspectives on Sport and Physical Education', one of the goals was to cover a range of international perspectives. This was a challenge because the PYD movement has its conceptual and empirical origins in the US. Indeed, the most influential writers on PYD (many of whom have contributed to this book) are based at US institutions. Nonetheless, research and practice from several nations have been addressed, including Canada, El Salvador, New Zealand, UK, and the US. Whereas these nations clearly do not reflect the global community, the authors have provided a variety of international perspectives.

## Organization

This book is intended as a resource for undergraduate students, graduate students, researchers, coaches, and other youth leaders who are interested in promoting positive developmental outcomes through sporting activities. Leading social scientists and program developers from a variety of disciplinary backgrounds (including developmental psychology, sport psychology, counseling, physical education, and pedagogy) were invited to contribute their perspectives in order to provide a thorough overview of PYD through sport. Whereas the main focus is the use of sport to promote PYD, related contexts (i.e. physical education and physical activity) and issues (i.e. social inclusion, youth disaffection, and peace education) have also been addressed.

This book is divided into three sections. It is important to distinguish between regular 'everyday' organized youth sport programs, which may or may not have any stated developmental goals, versus instructional programs which have stated goals consistent with the values of PYD. Accordingly, the first part of this book focuses more on organized youth sport programs, as opposed to specific instructional programs designed to promote PYD. These organized youth sport programs reflect the 'naturally occurring' sporting activities that youth around the world experience on a daily basis. In the second part instructional sport programs specifically designed to promote PYD are presented. Part 3 reflects a slight change of direction whereby each chapter focuses on complementary issues to PYD; namely social inclusion, youth disaffection, and peace education.

In Chapter 1, Nicole Zarrett and her colleagues report selected findings from the national longitudinal 4-H study of PYD being conducted out of Richard Lerner's lab at Tufts University (US). Professor Lerner is one of the leading proponents of PYD, and his conceptualization of the '5Cs' (competence, confidence, caring/compassion, character, and connection) underpin many sport PYD programs and research agendas. In Chapter 2, Nicholas Holt and Zoë Sehn discuss research conducted at the University of Alberta (Canada). This research has focused on describing and explaining adolescents' experiences in organized competitive sport, with a view to establishing what processes may be associated with producing positive (and negative) outcomes through involvement in this context.

The focus on organized youth sport continues in Chapter 3, where Jean Côté and his colleagues from Queen's University (Canada) provide a conceptual paper which integrates Côté's (1999) Developmental Model of Sport Participation with Bronfenbrenner's (2001) Ecological Systems Theory. Based on their synthesis of these theoretical perspectives and the empirical youth sport literature, they provide six suggestions for creating organized youth sport programs to promote PYD.

Part 2 includes instructional sport programs designed to promote PYD. These programs all originated in the US. In Chapter 4, Don Hellison and his colleagues provide an overview of their influential model of teaching personal and social responsibility, and focus specifically on the role of youth leadership in promoting PYD. In Chapter 5, Al Petitpas and his colleagues from Springfield College describe their framework for promoting PYD through sport. They focus on the role of mentorship within two instructional programs they have developed – the Play it Smart program for (American) football and the First Tee program for golf. The final chapter in this section, led by Christina Theokas (Virginia Commonwealth University), discusses Steve Danish's award-winning Going for Goal (GOAL) and Sports United to Promote Education and Recreation (SUPER) programs. The SUPER program has been delivered in Greece and New Zealand, and in the latter part of this chapter Ihirangi Heke describes his adaptation of SUPER (the Hokowhitu program) for New Zealand Māori youth.

Part 3 commences with Richard Bailey's (Roehampton University, UK) overview of issues relating to social inclusion and sport. His chapter draws from research conducted across several countries. In Chapter 8, Rachel Sandford and her colleagues from Loughborough University (UK) discuss their evaluations of two projects designed to positively influence disaffected youth through sport and physical activity. These projects (The Youth Sport Trust/BSkyB Living for Sport Project and the HSBC/Outward Bound Partnership Project) provide examples of how corporate and educational sectors can combine to positively influence youth development. In Chapter 9, James Mandigo and his colleagues from Brock University and the University of Toronto (Canada) provide a novel insight into their attempts to promote PYD and peace education through the creation of a national physical education program in El Salvador. This chapter also describes some unique ways of bringing together multiple stakeholders to promote PYD.

The final chapter by Nicholas Holt (University of Alberta, Canada) and Martin Jones (Loughborough University, UK) represents an attempt to draw together these unique contributions in order to establish what has been achieved so far, and where the field may go in the future. Overall, the contributions to this book reflect a vibrant and emerging area of scholarship that may ultimately help build on the popularity of youth sporting activities and create more pathways to positive developmental outcomes.

## References

Benson, P. L. (2003) 'Developmental assets and asset-building community: conceptual and empirical foundations', in R. M. Lerner and P. L. Benson (eds), *Developmental Assets and Asset-Building Communities: Implications for Research, Policy, and Practice*, pp. 19–43. Norwell, MA: Kluwer Academic.

Bronfenbrenner, U. (2001) 'The bioecological theory of human development', in N. J. Smelser and P. B. Baltes (eds), *International Encyclopedia of the Social and Behavioural Sciences*, vol. 10, pp. 6963–70. New York: Elsevier.

Catalano, R. F., Berglund, M. L., Ryan, J. A. M., Lonczak, H. S., and Hawkins, J. D. (1999) *Positive Youth Development in the United States: Research Findings on Evaluations of Youth Development Programs*. Washington, DC: Department of Health and Human Services.

Coleman, J., and Roker, D. (1998) 'Adolescence', *The Psychologist*, 11: 593–6.

Coles, B. (1995) *Youth and Social Policy*. London: UCL Press.

Côté, J. (1999) 'The influence of the family in the development of talent in sport', *The Sport Psychologist*, 13: 395–417.

Damon, W. (2004) 'What is positive youth development?' *Annals of the American Academy*, 59: 13–24.

Eccles, J., and Gootman, J. A., eds (2002) *Community Programs to Promote Youth Development*. Washington, DC: National Academy Press.

Graber, J., and Brooks-Gunn, J. (1997) 'Transitions and turning points: navigating the passage from childhood through adolescence', *Developmental Psychology*, 32: 768–76.

Hall, G. S. (1904) *Adolescence: Its Psychology and its Relations to Physiology, Anthropology, Sociology, Sex, Crime, Religion, and Education*, vols 1 and 2. New York: Appleton.

King, P. E., Schultz, W., Mueller, R. A., Dowling, E. M., Osborn, P., Dickerson, E., *et al.* (2005) 'Positive youth development: is there a nomological network of concepts used in the adolescent development literature?', *Applied Developmental Science*, 9: 216–28.

Larson, R. W. (2000) 'Toward a psychology of positive youth development', *American Psychologist*, 55: 170–83.

Larson, R., and Verma, S. (1999) 'How children and adolescents spend time across cultural settings of the world: work, play and developmental opportunities', *Psychological Bulletin*, 125: 701–36.

Lerner, R. M., Lerner, J. V., Almerigi, J. B., Theokas, C., Phelps, E., Naudeau, S., *et al.* (2005) 'Positive youth development, participation in community youth development programs, and community contributions of fifth-grade adolescents: findings from the first wave of the 4-H study of Positive Youth Development', *Journal of Early Adolescence*, 25: 17–71.

Offer, D. (1969) *The Psychological World of the Teenager*. New York: Basic Books.

Roth, J., Brooks-Gunn, J., Murray, L., and Foster, W. (1998) 'Promoting healthy adolescents: synthesis of youth development program evaluations', *Journal of Research on Adolescence*, 8: 423–59.

Steinberg, L. D. (1993) *Adolescence* (3rd edn). New York: McGraw-Hill.

Part I

# Organized sport programs and positive youth development

# 1 Variations in adolescent engagement in sports and its influence on positive youth development

*Nicole Zarrett, Richard M. Lerner, Jennifer Carrano, Kristen Fay, Jack S. Peltz, and Yibing Li*

## Introduction

Theory and research converge in pointing to the importance of structured out-of-school-time (OST) activities as important assets in the positive development of youth (Mahoney et al. 2005). Sports participation, the most ubiquitous OST activity (Larson and Verma 1999), has been associated with such positive indicators of development as higher academic performance in high school, greater likelihood of attending college, and greater autonomy and satisfaction in one's first job (Barber et al. 2001).

Yet, despite the recent surge of public and research interest in structured OST activities, less attention has been devoted to examining variations in participation (e.g. time spent in the activity) and how these variations may influence the nature of the relation between activity participation and adolescent functioning. Research has indicated that the amount of time youth spend participating in sports each week (intensity) (Simpkins et al. 2005), their participation stability/duration across adolescence (continuity) (Zaff et al. 2003), and the time they spend in other types of activities, in addition to their sports participation (Zarrett 2006), all play a role in how sports participation is linked to youth development.

In this chapter we explore the relation between sports participation and positive youth development (PYD). We focus on how this relation differs depending on the continuity and intensity of youth participation, as well as in relation to adolescents' distinct participation patterns across an array of structured activities.

## Sports participation and indicators of PYD

Youth participation in organized sports has been linked to indicators of adolescents' physical, social, psychological, and achievement-related behavior and development. Researchers (Barber et al. 2001; Eccles et al. 2003) found that, in comparison to non-participants, youth who participated in organized sports reported greater increases in liking school between 10th and 12th grades, received more frequent educational and occupational support, had higher academic performance in high school, had more total years of tertiary education by age 25, and attained a job at age 24 that offered autonomy and a promising future. These associations were not found with participation in art, community service, or school activities (Barber et al. 2001). Moreover, female athletes reported lower rates of sexual activity and/or early sexual intercourse, net of the influence of race, age, SES, quality of family relations, and participation in other extracurricular activities (Miller et al. 1998). Although research findings were mixd regarding the relation of sports praticipation and alcohol use, with some findings that suggested sport is associated with lower levels of alcohol use (Peretti-Watel et al. 2003), and other findings that indicated a positive relation between sports participation and alcohol use, participation in sports has been consistently linked to lower use of cigarettes, marijuana, cocaine, and 'other drugs' (Page et al. 1998), as well as lower rates of depression, and lower incidence of suicidal behavior.

The associations between sports participation and indicators of positive functioning also need to be considered in relation to more general findings about OST activities. Some evidence indicates that transient participation in an activity cannot foster the extent of activity-related gains that more sustained participation (continuity) affords young people (Mahoney et al. 2003). For example, in a nationally representative sample of 8th through 12th graders, Zaff et al. (2003) found that, after controlling for individual, parent, peer, and school-level variables, consistent extracurricular activity participation from 8th to 12th grade predicted academic achievement, prosocial behavior, and civic engagement in young adulthood (see also Mahoney et al. 2003).

Research has also found that the intensity of youth participation is important, so that those youth who spend more time in the activity benefit more than those who participate at lower levels or not at all (Simpkins et al. 2005; Cooper et al. 1999). One reason why continuity and intensity are thought to be major determinants of whether participation leads to desired benefits is because intense and continuous participation helps facilitate skill mastery and comprehensive knowledge (Larson et al. 2006). Similar to researchers in educational psychology, who assessed engagement as an indicator of the quality of a student's involvement with academic activities (Eccles et al. 1998), sports psychologists have also measured commitment to sport and intensity of participation as indicators of involvement quality (Scanlan and Lewthwaite 1986). Therefore, the time youth spend in an activity, along with their continuous participation over a number of years, are both ways to determine the level of youth commitment/engagement in the particular activity as well as the quality of the activity experience for the youth.

In addition, achievement-related decisions, such as the decision to try out for a sports team or spend time learning to play a musical instrument, are made within the context of a complex social reality that presents individuals a wide range of choices that have both immediate and long-term consequences (Eccles et al. 2003). That is, the more time an adolescent spends in one activity, the less time s/he has to devote to other types of activities. Thus, the decision to spend a great deal of time in an activity is, at least partially, fueled by a strong commitment/engagement in the particular activity. Therefore, in the current study we consider intensity of participation, not only as time invested in an activity (i.e. sports), but also as time invested relative to other available OST activities, in order to get a more accurate indication of a youth's level of commitment and involvement quality. It is also essential to address how youth are spending their out-of-school time across multiple activities because many youth participate in a variety of structured activities (Shanahan and Flaherty 2001; Theokas *et al.* 2006). Research suggests that what youth do in addition to their dominant activity can make a difference for youth development (Kleiber 1999).

## Patterns of OST activities

While the majority of previous research on participation in OST activities has typically focused on the implications of time devoted to a particular domain of activity, or the number of OST activities, less is known about how adolescents organize their out-of-school time across multiple domains. Recently, researchers using pattern-centered research methods have reported that patterns of participation across varying combinations of activities may be more strongly associated with positive development than participation in any one activity (Bartko and Eccles 2003; Shanahan and Flaherty 2001; Zarrett 2006). These approaches suggest that it is not necessarily the number of activities youth participate in, but rather particular combinations of activities, that help determine benefits from participation.

For example, pattern-centered research has found that some single-activity settings are related to a high level of functioning similar to that found for participation in a combination of OST activities. Bartko and Eccles (2003) reported that youth whose 11th grade extracurricular activities centered mainly around school-based clubs exhibited an overall pattern of high psychological and behavioral functioning that was similar to youth who were highly involved in a wide range of extracurricular activities, yet quite different from youth who were involved in a set of focused extracurricular activities characterized mainly by either sports or volunteer activities. Zarrett (2006) found that, although sports participation has been associated with lower rates of depression among youth (see also Barber *et al.* 2001), the combination of participation in sports and volunteering did not provide such a buffer for youth. Instead, participation in volunteering or sports exclusively was more beneficial to youth mental health than engagement in sports along with volunteering. In contrast, an activity pattern characterized by high participation intensity in both sports and school clubs was linked to the lowest rates of depression among all activity patterns examined, including a pattern of participation defined primarily by school clubs. These findings support the premise that different developmental trajectories result from differences in how youth spend their time across various activities. Therefore, in the current study we examined youth 7th grade activity participation profiles, with a focus on identifying the most effective sports-dominant participation patterns for promoting PYD.

In summary, the goals of the current study were to examine: (1) the relation of sports participation (as a dichotomous measure of participating or not participating) and concurrent well-being within 5th, 6th, and 7th grades and the influence of participation on well-being one year later; (2) the influence of continuous participation in sports across 5th, 6th, and 7th grades, as well as the intensity of youth participation at the 7th grade (time spent in sports) on indicators of adolescent functioning at Grade 7; and lastly, using a pattern-centered approach, (3) how the relation of sports participation and PYD may differ dependent on what types of additional activities youth participate in during their out-of-school time.

## The present study

This report is based on a subsample of 1122 of the original 3500 adolescents (56.8 percent female; 43.2 percent male) from the 4-H Study of Positive Youth Development (Lerner et al. 2005), and includes the sample of youth who participated in at least two of the first three waves of assessment (5th, 6th, and 7th grades). The mean age of youth at Wave 1 was 11 years (SD = .84 years). Because the autocorrelation for the family per capita income between the three waves was highly and significantly correlated (.81, .87, .89, $p < .001$), the average family per capita income was computed for each participant, based on available data in 1, 2, or 3 waves. The mean of this composite variable was \$14,685.76 (SD = \$9,079.68). In the current study we controlled for sex and (the square root of) average per capita family income in all analyses reported. The sample was largely European American (63.7 percent), but included some variation in race (Latino/a = 11.9, African American = 6.1, Asian American = 3.7 Native American = 2.3, Multi-ethnic/racial = 4.2, Other = 0.4 percent). Full details of the methodology of the 4-H Study have been presented in earlier reports (Jelicic et al. in press; Lerner et al. 2005).

We examined the relation of participation to various indicators of adolescent well-being. We first looked at overall PYD, shown to be a second-order latent construct constituted by psychological, behavioral, and social characteristics reflecting 'Five Cs': competence, confidence, character, connection, and caring. In turn, research suggests that among thriving youth a sixth C, contribution (e.g. to family, community) develops (Lerner et al. 2005). Therefore, we also examine the degree to which youth contributed to their families/communities (Contribution), measured as a composite score of twelve items divided into four subsets: leadership, service, helping, and ideology. Other indicators of functioning assessed included: participation in risk behaviors, defined by questions regarding both the frequency of substance use (e.g. alcohol) and other types of delinquent behaviors, such as how many times they had hit or beat up someone in the last year, and; depressive feelings (CES-D; Radloff 1977), such as 'how often they felt sad during the past week'. The construction, reliability, and validity of these measures are described in Lerner et al. (2005).

## Sport participation and youth development

Using a 2 (sex) × 2 (participation) between-subject fixed effects ANCOVA, with average family per capita income as the covariate, we examined the concurrent relation between participation in sports (using a dichotomous measure of youth participation in any community or school-related sport program) and indicators of PYD, contribution, risk behavior, and depression at the 5th, 6th, and 7th grade, as well as the predictive relation of participation on indicators of PYD measured during the consecutive year (e.g. 5th and 6th grade participation on 6th and 7th grade PYD, respectively). In all grades, in comparison to youth who did not participate, youth who did participate in sports reported significantly higher levels of PYD. At 5th Grade $F(3, 642) = 7.61, p < .01$, at 6th Grade $F(3, 1047) = 9.41$, $p < .01$, and at 7th Grade $F(3, 775) = 13.77, p < .001$. Similar differences existed for Contribution. At 5th Grade $F(3, 568) = 11.17, p = .001$, at 6th Grade $F(3, 1018) = 22.96, p < .001$, and at 7th Grade $F(3, 772) = 49.22, p < .001$. A significant interaction of participation and sex indicated that, at the 5th grade, participation in sports was related to higher levels of PYD primarily for girls, $F(4, 642) = 8.07$, $p < .01$; 5th grade boys did not differ in PYD in relation to their participation in sports. However, in the 6th and 7th grades, participation in sports was related to higher levels of PYD similarly for males and females. In addition, in the 5th grade participation in sports was related to lower incidences of risk behaviors for girls and the higher incidence of risk behaviors for boys; however, during the 6th and 7th grades no differences in risk behaviors were found between sports participants and non-participants by sex. These differences between participating and non-participating youth were found even after accounting for the variance explained by sex and socioeconomic background. There were no differences in youth reports of feeling depressed between sports participants and non-participants at any of the grades examined (see Table 1.1 for means).

Moreover, after accounting for the variance explained by sex and soicoeconomic status, participation in sports during 5th grade predicted higher PYD in grade 6, $F(3, 651) = 13.75, p < .001$, especially for female sport participants, $F(4, 651)$

*Table 1.1* Estimated marginal means of dichotomous sport participation on indicators of positive development

| Variable | Grade 5 M (SE) | | Grade 6 M (SE) | | Grade 7 M (SE) | |
|---|---|---|---|---|---|---|
| PYD | | | | | | |
| No sports participation | 73.68 | (.897) | 69.82 | (.798) | 68.29 | (.79) |
| Participates in sports | 76.66 | (.599) | 72.66 | (.465) | 71.80 | (.51) |
| Contribution | | | | | | |
| No sports participation | 39.92 | (1.013) | 41.50 | (.795) | 44.60 | (.84) |
| Participates in sports | 43.99 | (.671) | 45.93 | (.467) | 51.65 | (.55) |
| Risk Behavior | | | | | | |
| No sports participation | 1.02 | (.115) | 1.41 | (.128) | 1.54 | (.22) |
| Participates in sports | 0.98 | (.083) | 1.28 | (.078) | 1.55 | (.14) |
| Depression | | | | | | |
| No sports participation | 14.47 | (.570) | 13.35 | (.524) | 14.49 | (.65) |
| Participates in sports | 13.53 | (.405) | 12.44 | (.316) | 13.09 | (.42) |

Note:
All reported means and standard errors are net the effects of sex and average per capita family income.

Table 1.2 Dichotomous sports participation on indicators of functioning for subsequent waves

| Variable | Grade 5 to Grade 6 M (SE) | | Grade 6 to Grade 7 M (SE) | |
|---|---|---|---|---|
| PYD | | | | |
| No sports participation | 69.30 | (.868) | 68.51 | (.753) |
| Participates in sports | 73.27 | (.624) | 71.57 | (.458) |
| Contribution | | | | |
| No sports participation | 42.33 | (.882) | 44.94 | (.812) |
| Participates in sports | 46.15 | (.634) | 51.31 | (.494) |
| Risk Behavior | | | | |
| No sports participation | 1.35 | (.158) | 1.70 | (.209) |
| Participates in sports | 1.35 | (.112) | 1.56 | (.124) |
| Depression | | | | |
| No sports participation | 13.30 | (.586) | 13.69 | (.597) |
| Participates in sports | 12.06 | (.423) | 12.83 | (.366) |

Note:
All reported means and standard errors are net the effects of sex and average per capita family income.

$= 4.09$, $p<.05$, and it also predicted higher levels of Contribution, $F(3, 639) = 12.31$, $p<.001$, for all youth. In addition, 5th grade participation predicted lower incidences of risk behaviors for the girls and higher incidence of risk behaviors for the boys in 6th grade, $F(4, 747) = 5.65$, $p<.05$. Similarly, 6th grade sports participation predicted higher levels of 7th grade PYD, $F(3, 930) = 12.02$, $p = .001$, and Contribution, $F(3, 915) = 44.66$, $p<.001$ for all youth (see Table 1.2 for means). Similar to the previous grade, means suggest 6th grade participation was related to higher incidence of risk for boys and lower incidence of risk for girls during the 7th grade; however during the 7th grade this sex by participation interaction did not reach significance [$F(4, 856) = 3.70$, $p = .055$].

## Participation continuity

Although participation in sports was related to indicators of PYD, Contribution, and to some extent, lower risk behaviors, both concurrently and in consecutive grades, examination of participation stability/continuity suggests that this relationship differs depending on the number of years adolescents engage in sports activities [$F(4, 1022) = 11.96$, $p <.001$; $F(4, 1009) = 35.41$, $p <.001$; $F(4, 1014) = 3.11$, $p <.05$; for PYD, Contribution, and depression, respectively]. The results of 2 (sex) $\times$ 3 (participation) fixed effects ANCOVAs with average family per capita as a covariate indicated that, while youth who participated in sports for one year fared better on PYD and Contribution (SE $= 1.22$, $p = .001$) than youth who did not participate, their PYD scores were not significantly different than those of non-participants (SE $= 1.14$, $p =.554$). In contrast, youth who participated for two or more years had significantly higher PYD, SE $= 1.01$, $p<.001$, and Contribution, (SE $= 1.10$, $p <.001$)than non-participants and youth who participated for a single year (SE $= .87$, $p <.01$; SE $= .94$, p $<.001$; for PYD and Contribution,

Table 1.3 Continuity of participation on indicators of adolescent functioning

| Continuity of participation | PYD | | Contribution | | Risk Behavior | | Depression | |
|---|---|---|---|---|---|---|---|---|
| | M | SE | M | SE | M | SE | M | SE |
| No participation | 67.76[a] | .88 | 43.38[a,b] | .95 | 1.48 | .26 | 14.10 | .71 |
| One year | 69.27[b] | .73 | 47.90[a,c] | .77 | 1.92 | .21 | 14.28 | .58 |
| Two or more years | 72.21[a,b] | .50 | 52.22[b,c] | .54 | 1.59 | .24 | 12.69 | .41 |

Note:
Within a column, means with the same superscript (a, b or c) are significantly different according to Bonferroni post hoc tests, p < .05. All reported means and standard errors are net the effects of sex and average per capita family income.

respectively). Moreover, there was some indication that participation continuity was related to lower rates of depression, where youth who participated in sports for two or more years reported lower rates of depression than both non-participants and youth who participated for a single year (see Table 1.3 for means). There were no differences in 7th grade risk behaviors by participation continuity across 5th, 6th, and 7th grades.

## Participation intensity

Intensity of sports participation was measured as the total amount of time youth reported spending in community sports, school sports, and martial arts during the school year and subsequent summer. Similar to the analyses examining both dichotomous and continuous measures of participation, linear regression analyses, with participation intensity, sex, and average per capita income entered as predictors in the model, indicated that the more time youth spent participating in sports during the 7th grade, the higher their levels of PYD, $B = .678$, $\beta = .192$, $p < .001$, and Contribution, $B = 1.10$, $\beta = .289$, $p < .001$. In addition, the more time youth spent participating in sports, the lower their depression scores ($B = -.161$, $\beta = -.06$, $p = .05$). Participation intensity was not related to the level of youth engagement in risk behaviors, $B = -.802$, $\beta = -.008$, $p = .786$.

## Activity participation profiles

Finally, adolescents' 7th grade sports participation and indicators of PYD was explored using Cluster Analysis (Ward's method, Ward 1963). This pattern-centered approach enabled us to account for both adolescents' intensity of participation and their engagement in sport relative to their participation in other activities. We used a list of 17 activities that included youth development (YD) programs (e.g. 4-H, Boys and Girls Clubs), after-school clubs (e.g. school government, chess club), team and individual sports, the arts (e.g. music, drama), service (e.g. volunteering), and paid work. Youth reported the amount of time they spent participating in each activity during the current school year/summer (0 = never to 5 = every day). Time spent participating was standardized for each activity measured prior to cluster analysis.

Within the ten-cluster solution that emerged, we found three different types of sport-dominant participation profiles. In the first of these sports clusters youth were more involved in sports relative to their participation in other activities (they had lower than average reports of time spent in all other activities measured). For ease of presentation, this group of youth was referred to as the 'Sports-Only' Cluster, but the reader should keep in mind that a brief one or two word label cannot adequately capture the entire profile of activity involvement. The second sport cluster, 'Sport + YD,' is distinguished by high rates of participation in both sports and youth development programs, and by slightly above average time spent volunteering and in religious-based activities. The third sport cluster, which we named the 'High-Engaged' group, is characterized by spending above average time in all the activities measured. In fact, the time High-Engaged youth devoted to sport is similar to the amount of time Sport + YD youth spent in sports; both groups spent more time in sport than all others including the Sport-Only youth (see Table 1.4 for means). A fourth activity profile, 'Work + Religion,' involved youth who spent considerably less time devoted to sports in comparison to the other sport profiles, but was characterized by above average participation in sport relative to the non-sport profiles that emerged. Therefore, in our comparison analyses we also considered these youth as having another type of sport-dominant activity profile.

For our comparison analyses, the remaining youth from other activity profiles were combined and considered the 'Other-Activities' profile, with the exception of the 'Low-Engaged' youth, characterized by lower than average participation in all activities, and the 'Work' youth, characterized by above average involvement in paid work. Youth who had either of these types of activity profiles were examined separately because of previous research suggesting that youth who spend excessive time in paid work and those who spend little time in structured OST activities fare worse than other youth on indicators of positive functioning (e.g. Bachman and Schulenberg 1993; Zarrett 2006) (see Figure 1.1).

Using 2 (sex) × 7 (participation pattern) fixed effects ANCOVAs with average family per capita income as a covariate, differences between youth by their participation profiles were found for PYD, $F(8, 934) = 8.09$, $p < .001$, Contribution, $F(8, 929) = 25.63$, $p < .001$, and depressed feelings, $F(8, 928) = 3.24$, $p < .01$. Youth of all activity profiles reported similarly low incidence of risk behaviors. Post-hoc contrasts (Tukey) indicated that the High-Engaged youth were significantly higher on PYD than youth in all other activity profiles except for youth of the Sport + YD profile and the Work-Religion profile, who had similarly high levels of PYD. The Sport + YD youth were significantly higher in PYD than the Sport-Only, Work, and Low-Engaged groups and were similar in PYD to youth highly involved in other structured OST activities ('Other-Activities'). In contrast, the Sport-Only youth were significantly lower on indicators of PYD in comparison to youth of all other activity profiles, with the exception of the Work and the Low-Engaged youth, who had similarly low levels of PYD.

Table 1.4 Means and standard deviations of adolescents' 7th grade activity participation profiles

| | | | | | Cluster | | | | | | |
|---|---|---|---|---|---|---|---|---|---|---|---|
| Activity | High Engaged | Sport+YD | Sport | Work+Religion | School | Performing Arts | Arts & Crafts | Religion | Work | Low Engaged | Total |
| | (n=67) | (n=61) | (n=92) | (n=54) | (n=56) | (n=130) | (n=179) | (n=145) | (n=200) | (n=166) | (N=1150) |
| YD Programs | .82 (1.78) | 1.75 (.93) | -.54 (.36) | -.13 (.74) | -.30 (.62) | -.28 (.60) | -.30 (.59) | -.49 (.41) | -.34 (.58) | -.46 (.48) | -.19 (.89) |
| Sport | .84 (1.12) | .84 (.77) | .47 (.71) | .31 (1.06) | .10 (.93) | .07 (.91) | -.11 (.92) | -.24 (.80) | .09 (.93) | -1.14 (.16) | -.04 (1.00) |
| School | 2.17 (1.94) | -.29 (.43) | -.41 (.12) | -.33 (.44) | 1.54 (.70) | -.15 (.63) | -.11 (.69) | -.34 (.29) | -.35 (.26) | -.42 (.13) | -.06 (.94) |
| Performing Arts | .65 (1.06) | -.32 (.83) | -.76 (.45) | .32 (1.00) | -.38 (.81) | 1.06 (.52) | .28 (.94) | -.72 (.46) | -.16 (.92) | -.76 (.48) | -.11 (.97) |
| Arts & Crafts | .77 (1.19) | -.14 (.90) | -.65 (.20) | -.24 (.62) | -.64 (.25) | -.51 (.39) | 1.42 (.78) | -.58 (.34) | -.47 (.45) | -.64 (.18) | -.14 (.93) |
| Volunteer | 2.18 (1.78) | .24 (.80) | -.63 (.19) | .17 (.73) | -.48 (.37) | -.14 (.68) | -.04 (.72) | -.32 (.47) | -.04 (.84) | -.53 (.37) | -.07 (.96) |
| Religious | .64 (1.03) | .25 (1.03) | -.87 (-.10) | 1.24 (.75) | -.48 (.61) | .23 (.97) | -.12 (1.00) | .89 (.83) | -.60 (.48) | -.80 (.30) | -.08 (.99) |
| Paid work | .75 (1.11) | -.17 (.74) | -.61 (-.46) | 1.60 (.48) | -.34 (.76) | -.50 (.57) | -.20 (.84) | -.51 (.55) | .81 (.87) | -.75 (.37) | -.08 (.97) |

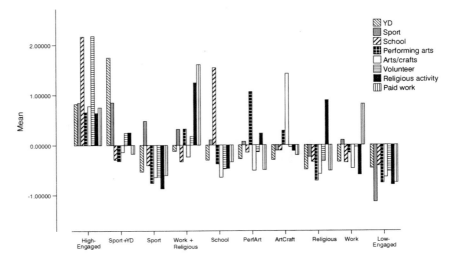

*Figure 1.1*   Youth 7th grade activity participation profiles

The High-Engaged youth and those youth who had a profile of Sports + YD reported similar levels of Contribution, significantly higher than youth in all other groups. In contrast, youth who participated primarily in sports ('Sport-Only') reported significantly lower levels of Contribution in comparison to youth in all other activity profiles, except for those who had a Low-Engaged activity pattern, who reported equally low levels of Contribution.

Although youth in the Sport-Only profile reported lower PYD and Contribution than youth in the other activity profiles, they reported significantly lower depression than both the High-Engaged and Low-Engaged youth. In fact, while Sport + YD youth were not different from any other group in their experiences with depression, High-Engaged youth were at greatest risk for experiencing depressed feelings (see Table 1.5 for means).

## Discussion

Researchers and youth advocates have proposed important benefits of sports involvement. However, to date, little research has accounted for the dynamic ways in which youth spend their free time. Accounting for such variation in participation will provide a more fine-grained understanding of the relation between youth activity participation and their functioning and, in turn, will help researchers and policy-makers effectively use sports as a tool in promoting PYD.

To date, researchers have grouped youth into two categories: youth who participate in OST activities and youth who do not (Simpkins 2003). We replicated previous research using a dichotomous measure of participation and various indicators of adolescent functioning, and found sports participation is, in most instances, beneficial for youth in both the concurrent and subsequent school

*Table 1.5* Means and standard deviations of adolescents' 7th grade activity participation profiles

| Clusters | PYD | | Contribution | | Risk Behavior | | Depression | |
|---|---|---|---|---|---|---|---|---|
| | M | SE | M | SE | M | SE | M | SE |
| High Engaged | 75.55 | 1.56 | 60.26 | 1.63 | 1.96 | .46 | 16.26 | 1.25 |
| Sport+YD | 74.44 | 1.68 | 57.42 | 1.76 | 1.24 | .51 | 14.53 | 1.39 |
| Sport | 67.88 | 1.37 | 43.82 | 1.44 | 1.54 | .42 | 11.96 | 1.15 |
| Work+Religious | 73.11 | 1.79 | 53.07 | 1.84 | 1.50 | .53 | 12.52 | 1.44 |
| School | 74.34 | 1.75 | 50.97 | 1.82 | 1.71 | .52 | 13.09 | 1.46 |
| Performing Arts | 72.16 | 1.15 | 50.90 | 1.20 | 1.39 | .34 | 12.73 | .93 |
| Arts/Crafts | 71.86 | .99 | 51.96 | 1.03 | 1.18 | .30 | 13.03 | .80 |
| Religious | 70.95 | 1.06 | 48.32 | 1.11 | 1.74 | .31 | 11.87 | .87 |
| Work | 70.05 | .91 | 49.65 | .95 | 2.02 | .27 | 12.58 | .76 |
| Low Engaged | 65.72 | 1.04 | 40.59 | 1.07 | 1.97 | .31 | 15.69 | .83 |

Note:

All reported means and standard errors are net the effects of sex and average per capita family income.

year. Our aim was to extend this research by considering how this relation differs dependent on variations in adolescent participation. Our findings suggest that there are nuances in this relation that are important for researchers and youth advocates to address. Specifically, although we found that participation predicted PYD, Contribution, and depression, youth only benefited from their involvement if their participation was intense and continued for more than a year. In addition, while dichotomous sports participation was related to fewer risk behaviors during the early adolescent years, when we considered the intensity and continuity of youth participation, sports participation was not predictive of risk behaviors. Such findings suggest that the link between sport participation and risk behaviors might be, in part, related to what types of youth select themselves into sport. At least during the early to middle adolescent years, those more "risky" youth who are drawn to sport, may simply participate with less intensity in the activity, and fail to persist in the activity for more than one year. However, with such small variance in risk behaviors during this early adolescent period, such interpretation of the findings is simply conjecture.

To further extend current research on the benefits of sports participation, we also examined how youth were spending their free time across multiple activities. In support of previous research (e.g. Zarrett 2006), we found differences between three distinct sports-dominant activity patterns common for youth in the 7th grade. First, similar to research that measured participation using an aggregate score of the number of activities youth participated in (Zaff et al. 2003), our findings indicated that youth highly engaged in a variety of activities (High-Engaged) were faring well on multiple indicators of positive functioning. Some researchers have proposed that participation in multiple OST activities is most beneficial for youth because engagement in such a variety of activities is presumed to provide access to a larger and more diverse group of social supports, the opportunity to master a variety of competencies, and to cope with challenging tasks (Mahoney 2000).

However, using a pattern-centered approach, that took into consideration various combinations of participation intensity across multiple activities, we found another sport-dominant activity pattern that was just as beneficial to youth as the High-Engaged pattern. Specifically, those youth who had a Sports + YD activity pattern fared just as well as the High-Engaged youth on all indicators of functioning.

In contrast, youth with the Sport-Only pattern reported lower PYD and Contribution than youth in all other OST activity patterns. These findings do not necessarily suggest that participation in sports alone is not effective for promoting PYD. Rather, a pattern-centered approach offers a fine-grained picture of those youth highly engaged in sports. Our findings suggest that there may be different types of youth who get involved in sports, and also different settings in which sports are offered. For example, without their sports participation, the Sport-Only activity profile resembled that of the Low-Engaged profile (see Figure 1.1). Moreover, even though their participation in sports was above average in comparison to non-sport dominant activity patterns, Sport-Only youth spent less time in sports relative to the other sport groups that emerged. Both features of this pattern may put these youth at a disadvantage.

Additional research that explores differences in these activity patterns by characteristics of the youth, and their families, schools, and neighborhoods is needed to gain better understanding of how activities contribute to PYD. For instance, economically disadvantaged youth are the least likely to participate in OST activities (Posner and Vandell 1999), and are often overrepresented in a Low-Engaged activity pattern (Zarrett 2006). Thus, it is likely that the Low-Engaged youth, and maybe youth who participated in the Work and Sport-Only patterns in our sample, come from homes, schools, and/or neighborhoods that have fewer resources to support PYD. If so, it is possible that participation in sports may function as a positive asset in the lives of those youth who would otherwise not be engaged in any OST activities. The lower rates of depression among youth of the Sport-Only group may be an indication of this positive influence.

This research may also help us to explain the higher rates of depression of youth in the High-Engaged activity pattern. Specifically, while engagement in multiple activities may expose youth to experiences that provide a strong backing for success, our findings suggested that High-Engaged youth report more symptoms of depression, at least during early adolescence. These findings may partially support the over-scheduling hypothesis, which proposes that the stress/pressure of too many activities may negatively influence the mental health of youth in early adolescence (Elkind 1967; Powell et al. 2002), even if there is not much support for this idea in later adolescence (Mahoney et al. 2006). However, we may have found differences in depression by activity participation patterns simply because the High-Engaged activity pattern consisted of a considerably high percentage of females (62.7 percent). Considerable research has found that heightened depression is common in girls during early and middle adolescence (e.g. Simmons and Blyth 1987).

Although we cannot fully disentangle the causal ordering among activity participation and positive functioning (see Eccles et al. 2003; Zarrett 2006), our longitudinal data will help us illuminate some of the effects of participation on development by enabling us (1) to examine within-person changes in the positive functioning of youth who get involved and stay involved in the sport-dominant activity patterns throughout the adolescent years, and (2) to take into account school, family, and youth assets/disadvantages linked to both adolescents' involvement in OST activities and their overall developmental trajectories.

Moreover, the sport setting may also be important for youth to benefit from their participation. For example, in contrast to the Sport-Only youth, the Sport + YD youth were likely participating primarily in the sport activities provided by their YD program (e.g. YMCA). YD settings are typically focused on providing youth with highly safe and structured environments, positive mentors, and positive overarching goals. For example, 4-H is a 'community of young people across America who are learning leadership, citizenship and life skills' (4-H website 2006), and the Boys and Girls Clubs focuses on 'promoting and enhancing the development of boys and girls by instilling a sense of competence, usefulness, belonging and influence' (Boys and Girls Clubs 2006). Therefore, future research should examine differences in the quality of the sport programs offered; these differences may also function to moderate the benefits of participation for youth.

The current study supports extant research on youth OST activities, which generally finds links between activity participation and PYD. Furthermore, it expands on this literature by examining some of the different facets of youth participation to better understand the most effective ways to promote PYD through participation in sports. Findings suggest that the relation between participation and adolescent functioning is complex. The careful study of detailed characteristics of youth participation, such as their intensity, continuity, and pattern of involvement across activities, proves important for researchers and policy-makers to identify the ways participation will be most beneficial to youth.

## Acknowledgements

The preparation of this chapter was supported in part by a grant from the National 4-H Council.

## References

Bachman, J. G., and Schulenberg, J. (1993) 'How part-time work intensity relates to drug use, problem behavior, time use, and satisfaction among high school seniors: are these consequences or merely correlates?', *Developmental Psychology*, 29: 220–35.

Barber, B. L., Eccles, J. S., and Stone, M. R. (2001) 'Whatever happened to the Jock, the Brain, and the Princess? Young adult pathways linked to adolescent activity involvement and social identity', *Journal of Adolescent Research*, 16: 429–55.

Bartko, W. T., and Eccles, J. S. (2003) 'Adolescent participation in structured and unstructured activities: a person-oriented analysis', *Journal of Youth and Adolescence*, 32: 233–41.

Boys and Girls Club of America (2006) *Our Mission*. Retrieved 9 Sept. 2006 from http://www.bgca.org/whoweare/mission.asp.

Cooper, C. R., Denner, J., and Lopez, E. M. (1999) 'Cultural brokers: Helping Latino children on pathways toward success', *Future of Children*, 9: 51–7.

Eccles, J. S., Wigfield, A., and Schiefele, U. (1998) 'Motivation to succeed', in W. Damon (series ed.), and N. Eisenberg (vol. ed.), *Handbook of Child Psychology*, vol. 3, *Social, Emotional and Personality Development* (5th edn), pp. 1017–94. New York: Wiley.

Eccles, J.S., Barber, B.L., Stone, M., and Hunt, J. (2003) 'Extracurricular activities and adolescent development', *Journal of Social Issues*, 59: 865–89.

Elkind, D. (1967) 'Egocentrism in adolescents', *Child Development*, 38: 1025–34.

Jelicic, H., Bobek, D., Phelps, E., Lerner, J. V., and Lerner, R. M. (in press) 'Using positive youth development to predict contribution and risk behaviors in early adolescence: findings from the first two waves of the 4-H Study of Positive Youth Development', *International Journal of Behavioral Development*.

Kleiber, D. A. (1999) *Leisure Experience and Human Development: A Dialectical Interpretation*. New York: Basic Books.

Larson, R., and Verma, S. (1999) 'How children and adolescents spend time across cultural settings of the world: work, play and developmental opportunities', *Psychological Bulletin*, 125: 701–36.

Larson, R. W., Hansen, D., and Moneta, G. (2006) 'Differing profiles of developmental experiences across types of organized youth activities', *Developmental Psychology*, 42: 849–63.

Lerner, R. M., Lerner, J. V., Almerigi, J. B., Theokas, C., Phelps, E., Naudeau, S., *et al.* (2005) 'Positive youth development, participation in community youth development programs, and community contributions of fifth-grade adolescents: findings from the first wave of the 4-H study of Positive Youth Development', *Journal of Early Adolescence*, 25: 17–71.

Mahoney, J. (2000) 'School extracurricular activity participation as a moderator in the development of antisocial patterns', *Child Development*, 71: 502–16.

Mahoney, J. L., Cairns, B. D., and Farmer, T. (2003) 'Promoting interpersonal competence and educational success through extracurricular activity participation', *Journal of Educational Psychology*, 95: 409–18.

Mahoney, J. L., Larson, R., and Eccles, J., eds (2005) *Organized Activities as Contexts of Development: Extracurricular Activities, After-School and Community Programs*. Hillsdale, NJ: Lawrence Erlbaum Associates.

Mahoney, J. L., Harris, A. L., and Eccles, J.S. (2006) 'Organized activity participation, positive youth development, and the over-scheduling hypothesis', *Social Policy Report*, 20(4): 3–31.

Miller, K. E., Sabo, D. F., Farrell, M. P., Barnes, G. M., and Melnick, M. J. (1998) 'Athletic participation and sexual behavior in adolescents: the different worlds of boys and girls', *Journal of Health and Social Behavior*, 39: 108–23.

National 4-H Headquarters (2006) Essential elements of 4-H. Retrieved November 9, 2006 from http://www.national4-hheadquarters.gov/about/4h_elements.htm.

Page, R. M., Hammermeister, J., Scanlon, A., and Gilbert, L. (1998) 'Is school sports participation a protective factor against adolescent health risk behaviors?', *Journal of Health Education*, 29: 186–92.

Peretti-Watel, P., Guagliardo, V., Verger, P., Pruvost, J., Mignon, P., and Obadia, Y. (2003) 'Sporting activity and drug use: alcohol, cigarette and cannabis use among elite student athletes', *Addiction*, 98: 1249–56.

Posner, J. K., and Vandell, D. L. (1999) 'After-school activities and the development of low-income urban children: a longitudinal study', *Developmental Psychology*, 35: 868–79.

Powell, D.R., Peet, S.H. and Peet, C.E. (2002) 'Low-income children's academic achievement and participation in out-of-school activities in 1st grade', *Journal of Research in Childhood Education*, 16(2): 202–11.

Radloff, L. S. (1977) 'The CES-D scale: a self-report depression scale for research in the general population', *Applied Psychological Measurement*, 1: 385–401.

Scanlan, T. K., and Lewthwaite, R. (1986) 'Social psychological aspects of competition for male youth sport participants: IV: predictors of enjoyment', *Journal of Sport Psychology*, 8: 25–35.

Shanahan, M. J., and Flaherty, B. P. (2001) 'Dynamic development of time use in adolescence' (special issue), *Child Development*, 72(2): 385–401.

Simmons, R. G., and Blyth, D. A. (1987) *Moving into Adolescence: The Impact of Pubertal Change and School Context*. Hawthorne, NJ: Aldine.

Simpkins, S .D. (2003) *Does Youth Participation in Out-of-School Time Activities Make a Difference?* (vol 9, no. 1). Cambridge, MA: Harvard Family Research Project. Available from http://www.gse.harvard.edu/hfrp.

Simpkins, S. D., Ripke, M., Huston, A., and Eccles, J. S. (2005) 'Predicting participation and outcomes in out-of-school activities: similarities and differences across social ecologies', *New Directions for Youth Development*, 105: 51–69.

Theokas, C., Lerner, J. V., Lerner, R. M., and Phelps, E. (2006) 'Cacophony and change in youth after school activities: implications for development and practice from the 4-H Study of Positive Youth Development', *Journal of Youth Development: Bridging Research and Practice*, 1(1). Retrieved 29 June 2006 from http://www.nae4ha.org/directory/jyd/about.html

Ward, J.H., (1963) 'Hierarchical grouping to optimize an objective function', *Journal of the American Statistical Association*, 58: 236–44.

Zaff, J. F., Moore, K. A., Papillo, A. R., and Williams, S. (2003) 'Implications of extracurricular activity participation during adolescence on positive outcomes', *Journal of Adolescent Research*, 18: 599–630.

Zarrett, N. (2006) 'The dynamic relation between out-of-school activities and adolescent development', unpublished doctoral dissertation, University of Michigan, Ann Arbor, MI.

# 2 Processes associated with positive youth development and participation in competitive youth sport

*Nicholas L. Holt and Zoë L. Sehn*

## Introduction

In June 2002 the Canadian Parliament passed Bill C-54 ('An Act to Promote Physical Activity and Sport'). The overall purpose of this Bill was to develop a national strategy to 'affirm the important role of sport in Canadian culture and society' (Canadian Law and Government Division 2002: 1). Similarly, the British government has broadened the definition of sport to provide a greater emphasis on physical activity for health (Department for Culture, Media and Sport/ Strategy Unit 2004). These political decisions reflect the notion that youth sport is now being internationally viewed in a population health context, rather than the traditional narrow view of youth sport as the breeding ground for the next generation of elite athletes (Fox 2004).

Concerns about youth inactivity and obesity were key factors influencing the international shift in how sport is viewed. Fewer than half of Canadian youth aged 5 to 17 are sufficiently active for optimal growth and development (Craig *et al.* 2001), and approximately one-tenth of Canadian children are obese and a third are overweight (Tremblay *et al.* 2002). The dual crises of inactivity and obesity are not unique to Canada. Similar trends have been reported among youth from many other countries (see Janssen *et al.* 2005). Not only are sedentary behaviors central to concerns over inactivity and obesity, but many popular sedentary behaviors (e.g. hanging out with friends, playing video games, or watching television) do little to foster cognitive, emotional, or social development (Larson 1994). These concerns have led researchers to suggest that leisure time should be spent in more productive ways, such as by participating in high-quality after-school programs that will facilitate positive development (e.g. Eccles *et al.* 2003). Youth sport may be one vehicle for providing programs that may foster positive youth development (PYD).

Despite the potential for PYD, participation in youth sport has actually been associated with positive *and* negative developmental outcomes (Eccles *et al.* 2003). Hansen *et al.* (2003) suggested that *competition* may be the key variable in producing both positive and negative outcomes through sport, and they concluded that 'competition may encourage the kind of self-evaluation and character building needed to contribute to the team goal but at the same time may limit the development of collaborative skills and expose youth to negative experiences that challenge their character' (p. 51). Given the critical role of competition, the focus of the present chapter was on competitive youth sport, and it is primarily dedicated to examining how competitive sport participation may provide a context in which youth experience developmental opportunities. By briefly reviewing opportunities for PYD through participation in competitive youth sport, and through a discussion of our own research, this chapter provides some answers to the question: what are some features of the processes by which PYD may be achieved through participation in competitive youth sport?

## Opportunities for PYD through competitive sport

One reason why sport is a compelling context for studying PYD is because of its incredible popularity among young people. For example, almost 2.2 million Canadian children (54 percent) (Corbeil 2000) and up to 35 million children in the United States (Weiss and Hayashi 1996) participate in community, school, or privately run sports programs. Sports account for the largest amount of US adolescents' leisure time (Larson and Verma 1999) corresponding to four to six hours per week of their time on average (Csikszentmihalyi and Larson 1984). Furthermore, set against trends of rising obesity and the reductions of physical activity in schools and unorganized settings, a counter-trend is that participation in organized youth sports appears to be increasing (Smith *et al.* 2004). For example, statistics from the Canadian Soccer Association (2005) show that total (i.e. youth and adult) registrations in organized soccer have risen from 483,686 in 1995 to 841,671 in 2004. The vast majority of this increase was due to increasing junior (i.e. under 18 years) registrations, and there were 714,671 junior soccer players (84.9 percent) registered in 2004. Similar trends have been reported in the UK, which have been attributed to increasing participation in lifestyle activities such as swimming, cycling, and tennis (Coalter 2004), along with increasing female participation in traditional team sports such as soccer (Sport England 2003).

Sport participation has been associated with a range of positive outcomes. Children who participate in youth sport have increased physical fitness, reduced body fat, and higher subsequent sport/physical activity participation during adulthood compared to children who do not participate in youth sport (Alfano *et al.* 2002; Perkins *et al.* 2004). Furthermore, when children participate in organized structured activities like sport they report higher levels of intrinsic motivation, effort, and concentration than when they watch television or socialize with friends (Larson 1994; Lowe Vandell *et al.* 2005). Sport also provides a context for adolescents to develop their identities and explore their emotions (Hansen *et al.* 2003).

Other positive outcomes associated with sport participation include reduced likelihood of engaging in risky sexual behaviors (Miller *et al.* 1998), protection against regular smoking (Audrain-McGovern *et al.* 2006), and positive educational and occupational outcomes (Barber *et al.* 2003; Marsh and Kleitman 2003). Sport participation also predicted high self-esteem among US female college students

(Richman and Shaffer 2000), protected against suicidal behavior (Brown and Blanton 2002), and partially mediated risks for depressive symptoms for Canadian grade 8–10 boys and girls (Boone and Leadbeater 2006). It should be noted that sport has been associated with some negative outcomes, including increased use of alcohol and smokeless tobacco (Rainey et al. 1996; Garry and Morrissey 2000). The issue of negative outcomes in sport is more thoroughly addressed in Chapter 10 of this book.

Although organized physical activity and sport programs are thought to provide opportunities for growth by promoting activities that may positively influence development, a comprehensive understanding of how these programs influence the development of children and adolescents remains elusive. Researchers have suggested that youth are more likely to experience PYD when organized programs involve opportunities for community involvement, skill-building activities, personal recognition, and positive relationships with adults (Roth and Brooks-Gunn 2003); however, the specific characteristics of *sport* programs (as opposed to other types of youth programs) that may promote PYD have yet to be thoroughly examined. The work recently conducted at the University of Alberta is designed to illuminate some of the processes that people associate with the production of both positive (and negative experiences) in youth sport. In the next section we present our theoretical orientation, followed by a discussion of some of our key findings to date.

## Developmental systems theory

From a developmental systems approach development is viewed as a process of systematic and successive change arising from dynamic relations between the developing person and the contexts in which s/he engages (Lerner et al. 2005a). Some major assumptions of developmental systems approaches relate to systematic change and relative plasticity, relationism and integration, embeddedness and temporality, generalizability limits and diversity (Lerner and Castellino 2002). Two of these assumptions – change and relationism – helped formulate the research we conducted at the University of Alberta. These concepts are briefly outlined below.

Developmental systems theory assumes that the potential for change exists across the life span (Baltes 1987). Systemic change is not limitless. It may be constrained by past history or contextual conditions. However, this potential for systemic change – or *relative plasticity* – is an important principle, because relative plasticity 'legitimates a proactive search in adolescence for characteristics of youth and of their contexts that, together, can influence the design of policies and programs promoting positive development' (Lerner and Castellino 2002: 124).

The bases for systemic change lie in relations that exist between multiple levels of human interactions and functioning. Incorporating principles of Bronfenbrenner's (1977, 2001) ecological approach, proximal influences include peer group and family influences, whereas more distal influences are public policy, governments, and economic systems. These levels are structurally and functionally integrated, thus requiring a systems view of the levels involved in human development (Lerner *et al.* 2005a).

Positive development is both the precursor and product of positive community involvement (Lerner *et al.* 2002). Proponents of the PYD approach believe that all youth possess inherent strengths that can be cultivated and that all young people have the potential for positive development (Lerner *et al.* 2005b). It follows that the creation of productive relations between young people and various aspects of their society can encourage positive and healthy developmental change. Lerner and Castellino (2002: 128) suggested that a key question for researchers is 'How do individual and contextual processes relate in constituting the process of developmental change in adolescence?'. Our own research has involved descriptive analyses of some features of the processes that may underpin adolescents' developmental experiences in sport settings.

## Methodological considerations

The majority of research examining connections between psychosocial outcomes and sport participation has been conducted using quantitative, correlational research designs. Whereas correlational designs can show relations between variables, they are limited in terms of explaining the processes that may contribute to these relations. In fact, it has been argued that sport programs have been treated as a 'black box' (Larson 2000). Specifically, researchers have demonstrated a tendency to examine outcomes associated with sport rather than looking inside the black box to examine what types of processes and interpersonal interactions influence development in these sport settings (Eccles and Templeton 2002; Hansen *et al.*, 2003; Larson *et al.* 2004). As Hansen *et al.* (2003) concluded: 'we have little scientific information, however, on the specific developmental processes that occur within youth activities' (p. 26). Thus, in our own research we have adopted a somewhat less traditional approach. Different types of qualitative methodologies have been used in an attempt to understand the inner workings of the black box of youth sport and to identify and examine some of the processes that may influence PYD in sport environments.

## Developmental experiences in sport

One of our first studies involved examining self-reported developmental experiences in sport (Holt *et al.* 2006a). Interviews with 40 former youth sport participants revealed a range of experiences which were coded into six themes generally consistent with findings of similar studies of adolescents in organized youth programs (e.g. Dworkin *et al.* 2003; Hansen *et al.* 2003). The most positive outcome related to learning initiative (i.e. learning to set and work towards goals). However, when it came to themes such as developing peer relationships, exploration and identity work, emotional self-regulation, and developing connections to an adult social network, participants reported a mixture of both positive and negative outcomes. Overall, positive outcomes were found to outweigh negative outcomes;

however, the results suggested that competitive sport may be 'naturally suited' for teaching initiative, teamwork and social skills, but less well suited for teaching exploration and identity work, emotional self-regulation, peer relationships and knowledge, and developing connections to an adult network and acquiring social capital.

Extending the analysis further we focused on the processes that appeared to produce these mixed experiences, which primarily related to participants' interactions with their parents and coaches. For example, participants reported that parents provided general *emotional support* without exerting undue pressure. Parents *promoted responsibility* and taught participants values relating to *sportspersonship*, and *emphasized fun*. Examples of *negative parental involvement* related either to parents being 'over protective' and restraining participation, or, alternatively, to parents not taking a great deal of interest in participants' sporting activities.

Participants reported that their coaches taught them about *persistence and effort*, *sportspersonship*, and emphasized *working together as a team*. Coaches also *provided feedback* and taught the athletes *coping skills*. However, despite these positive lessons, coaches also had a negative influence on participants' sporting experiences. One of the most widely cited negative processes was associated with coaches' *overemphasis on winning*. Participants also reported that coaches often engaged in too much *negative communication* (e.g. making negative comments during games). The final negative aspect relating to coach involvement was based on participants' view of *sport politics* (e.g. not being selected to play on a team because people thought that they came from the 'wrong' town). Overall, the findings of this study highlighted the crucial role that important adults (i.e. parents and coaches) play in producing these developmental experiences in sport. This study also demonstrated the importance of 'looking inside' the black box of youth sport.

## The role of the coach

Another study in this series involved direct observations and interviews using a case study of one coach and 12 players from a Canadian high school soccer team (Holt 2007). The athletics program at this high school had a stated policy of teaching positive outcomes through sport participation. Consequently, we examined student-athletes' developmental experiences over the course of a season. Central themes arising from the analysis related to initiative, respect, and teamwork.

In terms of initiative, the coach valued hard work and 'pushed' the student-athletes to extend themselves. He appeared to create a structure for the players to demonstrate initiative, rather than teaching them about taking initiative per se. It seemed that the student-athletes had already learned about working hard and taking responsibility – in fact, these may have been some of the reasons why they were selected to the team in the first place. Thus, the team was a venue for the expression of initiative rather than for learning initiative. Respect related to demonstrating respect (for teammates, the opposition, and the referee). Whereas the coach emphasized that the student-athletes show respect, our observations revealed that he did not always model these behaviors himself (e.g. during games he was observed arguing with the referee). Respect tended to be taught 'retroactively' in that players were punished for not demonstrating respect.

Teamwork was the only skill-set which student-athletes appeared to actually learn through their involvement on the team. It involved learning to work towards a common goal and communicating with each other. Teamwork was also the only theme which student-athletes thought transferred to other areas of their lives. In summary, it seemed that the student-athletes on this team experienced opportunities to express initiative and encountered issues associated with respect (in terms of demonstrating respect), but they appeared to learn about developing teamwork skills.

## Competitive youth sport settings and parental behaviors

A feature of our research with high school students was that parents were not extensively involved in the players' sport involvement. Our subsequent research focused on some of the ways in which parents may impact early adolescents' experiences in competitive sport (Holt *et al.* 2006b; Holt and Wall 2005). Although there is a range of specific types of parenting behaviors, most can be distinguished by two key dimensions; parental support and parental control (Barnes *et al.* 2000). Comments that convey nurturance, attachment, acceptance, cohesion, and love, such as offering praise, encouragement or giving physical affection, can be considered parental support. Comments and behaviors that reflect discipline, punishment, supervision, and monitoring represent parental control because they are intended to direct the child's behavior in a manner considered acceptable to the parent. Based on these distinctions, we conducted a study to identify and explain parents' verbal reactions to situations in competitive youth soccer.

Data were collected using interviews, diaries, and over 120 hours of direct observations of youth soccer games in the 10–14 years age categories. We found that parents' comments could be categorized into six themes: performance contingent feedback, encouragement, instruction, striking a balance, negative comments, and derogatory comments. We also found that parents' verbal reactions changed in relation to game circumstances. For example, the highest total volume and most controlling comments were made during close games (scores tied or one goal difference), between local rivals, during the final minutes of play. These findings illustrated the specific verbal reactions that may constitute parental over-involvement (i.e. controlling comments) versus appropriate involvement (i.e. supportive comments). We suspect that parents who engage in more supportive behaviors during competitive youth sport events may help to produce more positive experiences for their children. However, this conclusion is speculative, and further research is required to examine the relation between parents' behaviors and outcomes associated with PYD.

## Conclusion

Through our research we have begun to identify and explain some of the processes through which PYD may occur through competitive sport, and we have used a range of qualitative methodologies to reveal information in response to this objective. There are limitations to our studies, most notably that our findings have limited generalizability to other settings. As such, there is a need to embrace a diversity of research designs and methodologies to further study how to promote PYD through participation in competitive sport. Furthermore, we need to follow adolescents over extended periods of time and across other social contexts to understand about how sport participation may influence development. Nonetheless, the results of our research offer some alternative perspectives and, when combined with findings from traditional quantitative research, will contribute to furthering an understanding of PYD through participation in competitive youth sport.

One area which we have yet to thoroughly address is how peer interactions may influence PYD. Youth may experience a great deal of psychosocial development in terms of their interactions with peers in sport (Moran and Weiss 2006). Studies which include parents, coaches, and peers will shed more light on salient interpersonal processes that contribute to PYD. Ultimately, research which helps to further delineate the processes that contribute to positive (and/or negative) outcomes will be useful for providing guidance about how to utilize sport to best teach positive developmental outcomes (Danish et al. 2003).

To date, our PYD research in competitive sport highlights the fact that it is the way in which competitive sport programs are structured and delivered (by parents and coaches) that will influence adolescents' experiences. Appropriate peer interactions (e.g. learning to work together as a team) may also help to create conditions for PYD. We suspect that parents play an important role in providing a foundation for PYD among early adolescents, whereas peers and coaches are more important during middle and later adolescence (cf. Côté 1999). Our own findings provide some direction for the creation of interventions in competitive settings to promote PYD. That is, we suggest that effective intervention strategies for early adolescents will include parents because these important adults play a key role in structuring adolescents' developmental experiences in sport. Interventions targeted at older teenagers should focus on coach and peer interactions. We believe that the unique demands of competitive sport may provide a context for teaching certain life skills – when sporting experiences are structured and delivered appropriately.

## Acknowledgements

In preparing this chapter, Nick Holt was supported by an operating grant from the Social Sciences and Humanities Research Council of Canada, and a Population Health Investigator Award from Alberta Heritage Foundation for Medical Research. These sources of funding are greatly appreciated. We are also grateful to Dr. Jennifer Butters for her insightful comments on a previous draft of this chapter.

# References

Alfano, C. M., Kleges, R. C., Murray, D. M., Beech, B. M., and McClananhan, B. S. (2002) 'History of sport participation in relation to obesity and related health behaviors in women', *Preventative Medicine*, 34: 82–9.

Audrain-McGovern, J., Rodriquez, D., Wileyto, P., Schmitz, K. H., and Shields, P. G. (2006) 'Effect of team sport participation on genetic predisposition to adolescent smoking progression', *Archives of General Psychiatry*, 63: 433–41.

Baltes, P. B. (1987) 'Theoretical propositions of life-span development psychology: on the dynamics between growth and decline', *Developmental Psychology*, 23: 611–26.

Barber, B. L., Eccles, J. S., and Stone, M. R. (2003) 'What happened to the Jock, the Brain, and the Princess? Young adult pathways link to adolescent activity involvement and social identity', *Journal of Adolescent Research*, 16: 429–55.

Barnes, G. M., Reifman, A. S., Farrell, M. P., and Dintcheff, B. A. (2000) 'The effects of parenting on the development of adolescent alcohol misuse: a six-wave latent growth model', *Journal of Marriage and Family*, 62: 175–87.

Boone, E. M., and Leadbeater, B. J. (2006) 'Game on: diminishing risks for depressive symptoms in early adolescents through positive involvement in sports', *Journal of Research on Adolescence*, 16: 79–90.

Bronfenbrenner, U. (1977) 'Toward an experimental psychology of human development', *American Psychologist*, 32: 513–32.

Bronfenbrenner, U. (2001) 'The bioecological theory of human development', in N. J. Smelser and P. B. Baltes (eds), *International Encyclopedia of the Social and Behavioural Sciences*, vol. 10, pp. 6963–70. New York: Elsevier.

Brown, D. R., and Blanton, C. J. (2002) 'Physical activity, sports participation, and suicidal behavior among college students', *Medicine and Science in Sports and Exercise*, 34: 1087–96.

Canadian Law and Government Division (2002) *Bill C-54: An Act to Promote Physical Activity and Sport*. Ottawa, ON: Parliamentary Research Library. Retrieved 4 Sept. 2004 from http://www.parl.gc.ca/37/1/parlbus/chambus/house/ bills/summaries/c54-e.pdf

Canadian Soccer Association (2005) *Player Demographics 2004*. Retrieved 22 Dec. 2006 from http://www.canadasoccer.com/eng/docs/2005_demographics.pdf

Coalter, F. (2004) 'Future sports or future challenges to sport?', in Sport England (ed.), *Driving up Participation: The Challenge for Sport*, pp. 77–84. London: Sport England.

Corbeil, J. P. (2000) 'Sport participation in Canada', *Canadian Social Trends*, 3: 212–17.

Côté, J. (1999) 'The influence of the family in the development of talent in sports', *The Sport Psychologist*, 13: 395–417.

Craig, C. L., Cameron, C., Russell, S. J., and Beaulieu, A. (2001) *Increasing Physical Activity: Supporting Children's Participation*. Ottawa, ON: Canadian Fitness and Lifestyles Research Institute.

Csikszentmihayli, M., and Larson, R. W. (1984) *Being Adolescent*. New York: Basic Books.

Danish, S. J., Taylor, T., and Fazio, R. (2003) 'Enhancing adolescent development through sport and leisure', in G. R. Adams and M. Berzonsky (eds), *Handbook on Adolescence*, pp. 92–108. Malden, MA: Blackwell.

Department for Culture, Media and Sport/Strategy Unit (2004) *Game Plan: A Strategy for Delivering Government's Sport and Physical Activity Objectives*. London: The Stationery Office.

Dworkin, J. B., Larson, R. W., and Hansen, D. (2003) 'Adolescents' accounts of growth experiences in youth activities', *Journal of Youth and Adolescence*, 32: 17–26.

Eccles, J. S., and Templeton, J. (2002) 'Extracurricular and other after-school activities for youth', *Review of Education*, 26: 113–80.

Eccles, J. S., Barber, B. L., Stone, M., and Hunt, J. (2003) 'Extracurricular activities and adolescent development', *Journal of Social Issues*, 59: 865–89.

Fox, K. R. (2004) 'Tackling obesity in children through physical activity: a perspective from the United Kingdom', *Quest*, 56: 28–40.

Garry, J. P., and Morrissey, S. L. (2000) 'Team sports participation and risk-taking behaviors among a biracial middle school population', *Clinical Journal of Sports Medicine*, 10: 185–90.

Hansen, D. M., Larson, R. W., and Dworkin, J. B. (2003) 'What adolescents learn in organized youth activities: a survey of self-reported developmental experiences', *Journal of Research on Adolescence*, 13: 25–55.

Holt, N. L. (2007) 'An ethnographic study of positive youth development on a high school soccer team', paper presented at Society for Research in Child Development conference, Boston, MA.

Holt, N. L., and Wall, M. P. (2005) 'Positive youth development through sport? Families' perceptions of their involvement in youth sport', paper presented at the Association for the Advancement of Applied Sport Psychology Conference. Vancouver, BC.

Holt, N. L., Black, D. E., and Tink, L. (2006a) 'Do athletes learn life skills through sport?', paper presented at Association for the Advancement of Applied Sport Psychology Conference, Miami, FL.

Holt, N. L., Tamminen, K. A., Sehn, Z. L., and Black, D. E. (2006b) 'Parental communication during youth soccer games', paper presented at SCAPPS conference, Halifax, NS.

Janssen, I., Katzmarzyk, P. T., Boyce, W. F., Vereecken, C., Milvihill, C., et al. (2005). 'Comparison of overweight and obesity prevalence in school-aged youth from 34 countries and their relationships with physical activity and dietary patterns', *Obesity Reviews*, 6: 123–32.

Larson, R. W. (1994) 'Youth organizations, hobbies, and sports as developmental contexts', in R. K. Silberiesen and E. Todt (eds), *Adolescence in Context*, pp. 46–65. New York: Teachers College Press.

Larson, R. W. (2000) 'Toward a psychology of positive youth development', *American Psychologist*, 55: 170–83.

Larson, R., and Verma, S. (1999) 'How children and adolescents spend time across cultural settings of the world: work, play and developmental opportunities', *Psychological Bulletin*, 125: 701–36.

Larson, R. W., Jarrett, R., Hansen, D., Pearce, N., Sullivan, P., Walker, K., Watkins, N., and Wood, D. (2004) 'Organized youth activities as contexts for positive development', in A. Linley and S. Joseph (eds), *Positive Psychology in Practice: From Research to Application*, pp. 540–60. New York: Wiley.

Lerner, R. M., and Castellino, D. R. (2002) 'Contemporary developmental theory and adolescence: developmental systems and applied developmental science', *Journal of Adolescent Health*, 31: 122–35.

Lerner, R. M., Bretano, C., Dowling, E. M., and Anderson, P. N. (2002) 'Positive youth development: thriving as a basis of personhood and civil society', in C. S. Taylor, R. M. Lerner, and A. von Eye (eds) and G. Noam (series ed.), *New Directions for Youth Development: Theory Practice and Research: Pathways to Positive Youth Development among Gang and Non-Gang Members*, pp. 11–33. San Francisco: Jossey-Bass.

Lerner, R. M., Brown, J. D., and Kier, C. (2005a) *Adolescence: Development, Diversity, Context, and Application* (Canadian edn). Toronto: Pearson.

Lerner, R. M., Lerner, J. V., Almerigi, J. B., Theokas, C., Phelps, E., Naudeau, S., *et al.* (2005b) 'Positive youth development, participation in community youth development programs, and community contributions of fifth-grade adolescents: findings from the first wave of the 4-H study of Positive Youth Development', *Journal of Early Adolescence*, 25: 17–71.

Lowe Vandell, D., Shernoff, D. J., Pierce, K. M., Bolt, D. M., Dadisman, K., and Brown, B. B. (2005) 'Activities, engagement, and emotion in after-school programs (and elsewhere)', *New Directions for Youth Development*, pp. 121–9. San Francisco: Jossey-Bass.

Marsh, H. W., and Kleitman, S. (2003) 'School athletic participation: mostly gain with little pain', *Journal of Sport and Exercise Psychology*, 25: 205–28.

Miller, K. E., Sabo, D. F., Farrell, M. P., Barnes, G. M., and Melnick, M. J. (1998) 'Athletic participation and sexual behavior in adolescents: the different worlds of girls and boys', *Journal of Health and Social Behavior*, 39: 108–23.

Moran, M. M., and Weiss, M. R. (2006) 'Peer leadership in sport: links with friendship, peer acceptance, psychological characteristics, and athletic ability', *Journal of Applied Sport Psychology*, 18: 97–113.

Perkins, D. F., Jacobs, J. E., Barber, B. L., and Eccles, J. S. (2004) 'Childhood and adolescent sports participation as predictors of participation in sports and physical fitness activities during young adulthood', *Youth and Society*, 35: 495–520.

Rainey, C. J., McKeown, R. E., Sargent, R. G., and Valois, R. F. (1996) 'Patterns of tobacco and alcohol use among sedentary, exercising, nonathletic, and athletic youth', *Journal of School Health*, 66: 27–32.

Richman, E. L., and Shaffer, D. R. (2000) '"If you let me play sports": how might sport participation influence the self-esteem of female adolescents?', *Psychology of Women Quarterly*, 24: 189–99.

Roth, J. L., and Brooks-Gunn, J. (2003) 'What exactly is a youth development program? Answers from research and practice', *Applied Developmental Science*, 7: 94–111.

Smith, A., Green, K., and Roberts, K. (2004) 'Sports participation and the obesity/health crisis', *International Review for the Sociology of Sport*, 39: 457–64.

Sport England (2003) *Young People and Sport in England 2002*. London: Sport England.

Tremblay, M. S., Katzmarzyk, P. T., and Willms, J. D. (2002) 'Temporal trends in overweight and obesity in Canada, 1981–1996', *International Journal of Obesity Related Metabolic Disorders*, 26: 538–43.

Weiss, M. R., and Hayashi, C. T. (1996) 'The United States', in P. De Knop, L. M. Engström, B. Skirstad, and M. R. Weiss (eds), *Worldwide Trends in Youth Sport*, pp. 43–57. Champaign, IL: Human Kinetics.

# 3 Participation, personal development, and performance through youth sport

*Jean Côté, Leisha Strachan, and Jessica Fraser-Thomas*

## Introduction

Youth sport has the potential to accomplish three important objectives in children's development (Côté and Fraser-Thomas 2007). First, sport programs can provide youth with opportunities to be physically active, which in turn can lead to improved *physical health*. Second, youth sport programs have long been considered important to youth's *psychosocial development*, providing opportunities to learn important life skills such as cooperation, discipline, leadership, and self-control. Third, youth sport programs are critical for the learning of *motor skills*; these motor skills serve as a foundation for recreational adult sport participants as well as future national sport stars.

Currently, youth sport programs are not producing outstanding results in any of these three objective areas. For example, child obesity rates in developed nations are high (e.g. Tremblay *et al.* 2002), while problem behaviors such as drug use and delinquency are on the rise among youth (e.g. Health Canada 2004). Further, attrition rates from youth sport programs are extremely high during adolescence, with an estimated one-third of all participants between 10 and 17 years of age withdrawing from sport programs every year (Gould 1987), leading sport psychology researchers to identify dropout as an area of concern (Brustad *et al.* 2001). In this chapter, we outline some of the current youth sport research and discuss youth sport participation within a broader integrated developmental and ecological model.

## The developmental model of sport participation

Côté and colleagues' Developmental Model of Sport Participation (DMSP: Côté 1999; Côté and Fraser-Thomas 2007; Côté and Hay 2002) provides a framework with pathways that support continued participation for all youth, health benefits, and psychosocial development through sport. The DMSP emerged from extensive retrospective interviews with athletes in a variety of sports (e.g. hockey, baseball, gymnastics, rowing, tennis, and triathlon) and proposes three possible sport participation trajectories: 1) recreational participation through sampling, 2) elite performance through sampling, and 3) elite performance through early specialization. Two of these trajectories, recreational participation and elite performance through sampling, have the same foundation from ages 6 to 12. After the sampling years, sport participants may choose to either stay involved in sport at a recreational level (*recreational years*, age 13+) or embark on a path that focuses primarily on performance (*specializing years*, age 13–15; *investment years*, age 16+). These two trajectories have different outcomes in terms of performance, but similar psychosocial and physical health benefits. The third possible trajectory is elite performance through early specialization. While this path often leads to elite performance, it may also lead to some negative physical and psychosocial outcomes.

## Trajectory 1: Recreational participation through sampling

During the sampling years (age 6–12), athletes participate in a variety of sports with the focus being primarily on deliberate play activities. Côté and colleagues (Côté and Hay 2002; Côté *et al.* 2003) define deliberate play activities in sport as those designed to maximize inherent enjoyment. These activities are regulated by flexible age-adapted rules, and are set up and monitored by children or an involved adult. Children typically modify rules to find a point where their game most resembles the actual sport, but still allows for play at their level. These years are considered essential building blocks for recreational sport participation. The recreational years (age 13+) are usually seen as an extension of the sampling years, with the primary goals being enjoyment and health. Activities involve more deliberate play than deliberate practice. Deliberate practice is defined as highly structured activity that requires effort, generates no immediate rewards, and is motivated by the goal of improving performance rather than inherent enjoyment (Ericsson *et al.* 1993). During the sampling and recreational years, coaches are primarily supportive and encouraging. The roles of the parents during the sampling and recreational years include introducing their children to sports, enrolling them in diverse activities, and providing them with necessary resources, equipment, and playing opportunities. Parents should also provide adequate levels of emotional, informational, and tangible support to maintain their children's involvement in sport throughout development (Côté 1999).

## Trajectory 2: Elite performance through sampling

For youth interested in a more performance-oriented path, a second trajectory of the DMSP suggests that specialization begins around age 13, after the sampling years. The specializing years (age 13–15) are seen as a transitional stage to the investment years (age 16+). During the specializing years, youth engage in fewer activities, which are a mix of deliberate play and deliberate practice activities, while during the investment years, youth commit to only one activity, and engage primarily in deliberate practice. A recent review of retrospective studies of elite level athletes in various sports (Côté *et al.* 2007) show that this trajectory is a common pathway to elite performance for sports in which peak performance is achieved after puberty. During both the specializing and investment years, a more reciprocal coach–athlete respect develops, with coaches' styles becoming more skill-oriented and technical. Parents become less involved, but provide more financial and emotional support by helping their children through challenges and obstacles. Essentially, parents progress from a leadership role during the sampling years to a following and supporting role during the specializing and investment years (Côté 1999).

### Trajectory 3: Elite performance through early specialization

In sports where peak performance is achieved before puberty (e.g. women's gymnastics, figure skating), early specialization is often necessary to reach elite performance. This phenomenon is also being extended to a variety of other sports (namely baseball and basketball) as the attractiveness of post-secondary athletic scholarships become increasingly lucrative (Gould and Carson 2004). However, studies that examine the development of elite athletes in sports such as basketball and baseball do not support an early specialization trajectory towards elite performance (see Côté et al. 2007, for a review). The early specialization path is characterized by high volumes of deliberate practice and low amounts of deliberate play in a context that focuses on performance. Thus, elite performers in these 'early specialization' sports usually skip the sampling years, and consequently may experience some negative physical and psychosocial outcomes during this period. For example, 'early specializers' often experience overuse injuries, reduced sport enjoyment and are more likely to eventually drop out of the sport they originally specialized in. Wall and Côté (2007) showed that young elite dropout ice hockey players began off-ice training (for the purpose of improving hockey performance) at a younger age and invested significantly more hours per year in off-ice training at ages 12–13 than a group of invested young elite ice hockey players. These results, along with the results of other qualitative studies of dropout and burnout athletes (e.g. Carlson 1988; Gould et al. 1996), indicate that engaging in more sport-specific training activities at a young age may have negative implications for long-term sport participation.

When a child's overall development is considered, many environmental factors can also impact on an individual's sport participation trajectory. García Bengoechea and Johnson state that '[U]nderstanding the forces that facilitate sports participation may contribute to the development and implementation of effective programs that increase involvement in sport activities, thereby enhancing physical, social, and psychological wellness in children' (2001: 20). The environment, therefore, becomes an important and interesting component to explore when examining youth sport developmentally. Bronfenbrenner's ecological theory (1977, 1999) provides an integrated approach to studying the development of youth through sport participation.

## Ecological systems theory

Ecological systems theory refers to the notion that human development and human behavior are the materialization of person–context interactions (Bronfenbrenner 1995). Bronfenbrenner (1977) first conceptualized four nested systems (or levels) within an ecological network: 1) microsystem, 2) mesosystem, 3) exosystem, and 4) macrosystem. The first level, or microsystem, is comprised of participants, a physical domain, a location, and/or a program of activities. The second level, or mesosystem, is based on interrelationships between two or more microsystems involving the developing person (i.e. relationship between the coach and child). The third level, or exosystem, does not include the developing person within it; this level is representative of situations that affect the setting containing the person in question (i.e. interaction between coach and administrator). Lastly, the macrosystem includes cultural and social forces that impact human development. These nested systems are in constant interaction with each other to result in specific developmental processes and outcomes.

Bronfenbrenner later consolidated these ideas to form two specific propositions (1999). Proposition 1 postulates that human development, particularly in its early phases, occurs through processes of complex, reciprocal interactions between an active human organism and persons, objects, and symbols in its immediate environment. These interactions, or 'proximal processes', must occur on a regular basis and over a long period of time. Examples of patterns of these proximal processes include group or solitary play, reading, learning new skills, and athletic activities. Proposition 2 expands upon the nature of the proximal processes. This proposition states that the form, power, content, and direction of the proximal processes affecting development vary systematically as a joint function of: 1) the characteristics of the developing person, 2) the environment in which the processes are happening, 3) the developmental outcomes under consideration, and 4) the changes occurring over the time period in which the processes are taking place. This approach is aptly named the process–person–context–time (PPCT) model.

## Linking the PPCT model to sport development

In this section we use the PPCT model to serve as a framework to further enhance understanding of healthy development through sport. In particular, components of the PPCT are integrated with concepts from the DMSP.

### Process

It has been suggested that proximal processes are a critical catalyst for human development, acting as mechanisms of organism–environment interaction (Bronfenbrenner 1995). We suggest two proximal processes principles to promote positive youth development in sport, in accordance with the DMSP. First, we suggest a progression from deliberate play activities during childhood to progressively more deliberate practice activities during adolescence. Deliberate play activities during childhood will help children become more self-directed towards their participation in sport (Ryan and Deci 2000; Vallerand 2001). Furthermore, deliberate play situations allow children the freedom to experiment with different movements and tactics, and the opportunity to learn to innovate, improvise, and respond strategically. Further, deliberate play activities in sport allow children to perfect skills that would not be practiced in organized situations (Côté *et al.* 2007). However, during adolescence it becomes more important to integrate deliberate practice activities into regular scheduling, particularly in elite sport programs.

Second, we suggest that children have the opportunity to sample various sporting activities. Sampling during childhood allows individuals to experience the context of various sports. For example, the proximal processes involved in basketball, soccer, tennis, golf, and track and field have distinctive features that can potentially lead to very different sport experiences and outcomes. We propose that sampling various sports allows individuals to establish different relationships with coaches, teammates, and other adults that have the potential to positively shape the course of development of youth.

## Person

The second component of the PPCT focuses on the person as both a producer and product of his or her environment; this component of the model draws attention to the variation in characteristics of individuals involved in sport. Characteristics such as self-perceptions and motivation have been examined extensively in youth sport research (Horn 2004; Weiss and Williams 2004). Fraser-Thomas *et al.* (2005) integrate concepts of the DMSP related to the 'person' with Benson's (1997) forty developmental assets. The assets fall into two broad categories: external and internal. Within each of these categories, four types of assets exist. External assets include: support, empowerment, boundaries and expectations, and constructive use of time. Internal assets reflect an individual's values and beliefs and include commitment to learning, positive values, social competencies, and positive identity. The forty developmental assets are commonly termed the 'building blocks' for human development (Benson 1997). The more developmental assets an adolescent possesses, the greater his or her likelihood of developing in a positive and healthy manner (Benson *et al.* 1998; Scales and Leffert 1999). Although no single activity can promote all developmental assets, Fraser-Thomas *et al.* (2005) recently contended that participation in sport can be an important activity for the acquisition of several developmental assets.

Despite these claims, it has been suggested that sport is not necessarily the 'magic ingredient' to the further development of positive youth, adding that sport and other leisure activities are capable of having both positive and negative influences on development of an individual (Danish *et al.* 2004). In fact, Mahoney and Stattin (2000), in their examination of adolescents' low-structured and high-structured sport and leisure activities, found that it was the structure and context of the activities rather than the activity itself that determined whether the outcomes were positive or negative in terms of adolescent development. Programs that focus on developmental assets integrate a broad range of individuals' internal and external attributes and increase the likelihood of healthy development through sport. Therefore, sport has the potential to contribute to a person's positive developmental outcomes if delivered within an appropriate framework such as the developmental assets framework.

## Context

Programs must also be delivered in an appropriate context, the third component of the PPCT model. This component refers not only to the developing person's physical environment but also to the individuals within that environment who form strong bonds and relationships with the developing person (Bronfenbrenner 1999). After examining the impact of the physical environment on youth, the National Research Council Institute of Medicine (NRCIM 2002, 2004) suggested eight main features that should be present in the context of community programs in order to facilitate positive youth development. These features are gaining increasing support from youth sport research (e.g. Fraser-Thomas *et al.* 2005) as they offer additional understanding of the context in which youth sport should be promoted.

### 1. Physical and psychological safety

Physical and psychological safety in youth sport settings refers to the existence of safe and healthy facilities and practices that encourage secure and respectful peer interactions. Research indicates that the athlete–peer microsystem has an impact on the child's sense of physical self-worth (Vazou *et al.* 2006) and on the adolescent's perceived competence and self-evaluations (Horn 2004). Therefore, it is important that peer interactions are respectful in sport in order to build confidence in youth and allow them to enjoy their participation in sport.

### 2. Appropriate structure

This feature suggests the existence of clear and consistent expectations regarding rules and boundaries. The DMSP provides some guidelines for the structure of youth sport programs (e.g. a shift in focus from deliberate play during childhood to deliberate practice during adolescence). Thus one could contend that providing activities that are properly structured has the potential to develop positive, well-adjusted, and optimistic youth.

### 3. Supportive relationships

The third setting feature relates to strong support, positive communication, and connectedness. A coach can influence a child's perceived competence, enjoyment, and motivation (Black and Weiss 1992) and play a role in a child's psychological, social, and physical growth (Conroy and Coatsworth 2006; Côté and Fraser-Thomas 2007). Training coaches about basic principles of positive youth development is likely to result into better youth sport programs and sporting environments that promote supportive relationships (Conroy and Coatsworth 2006; Smoll and Smith 1996).

### 4. Opportunities to belong

The fourth setting feature highlights the importance of meaningful inclusion, social engagement, and cultural competence in youth sport programs. Feeling a sense of belonging (i.e. being part of a team, developing friendships) is important in maintaining a child's motivation and interest in sport (Allen 2003). Healthy relationships can be encouraged by coaches who build a sense of team unity and cohesion.

### 5. Positive social norms

This feature relates to the development of values and morals rather than antisocial and reckless behaviors. Although a growing body of literature highlights some of the potential negative social norms associated with youth sport participation (e.g. violence, aggression, poor sportspersonship, and low morality reasoning: Bredemeier 1995; Lemyre *et al.* 2002), youth sport programs have the potential to develop positive values such as fair play, sportspersonship, cooperation, assertion, responsibility, empathy, and self-control (Côté 2002).

### 6. Support of efficacy and mattering

The sixth setting feature focuses on the importance of empowering youth and supporting their autonomy as they work to build their community. Research in sport emphasizes the need for coaches to develop autonomous athletes; giving youth the opportunity to choose their level of involvement in sport or contribution within a sport will empower them and also increase their intrinsic motivation for sport (Mallett 2005; Vallerand and Rousseau 2001).

### 7. Opportunities for skill building

The seventh setting feature emphasizes the importance of learning experiences. As previously outlined, sampling a variety of different sports through early diversification provides this opportunity, as youth have the chance to learn a variety of sport skills and are able to meet and interact with a variety of different people (i.e. peers, coaches). Furthermore, deliberate play and deliberate practice activities afford children and adolescents the opportunity to grow and develop their motor skills in appropriate settings.

*8. Integration of family, school, and community efforts*

This feature promotes the melding of the young person's environments to increase communication and lessen conflicts and dissonance. In youth sport, parents play a key role in athletes' development of other supportive relationships, such as coach–athlete interactions (Jowett and Timson-Katchis 2005). Further, the structure and environment of a community appear to play a role in youth's persistence and progression in sport, given research suggesting that smaller cities tend to produce more professional athletes (Côté *et al.* 2007).

### Time

Time is the last and often neglected component of the PPCT model. According to García Bengoechea and Johnson (2001), human development can only be fully understood if it is examined over an extended period of time. Thus, in order to truly comprehend child development in sport, individual attributes and their environmental interactions must be studied over time. The DMSP outlines how different activities benefit children's development at different ages, and provides a temporal progression of sport involvement with stages that are qualitatively and quantitatively different from each other. The first two trajectories (i.e. recreational participation through sampling and elite performance through sampling) include activities and environments that are similar during childhood and progressively different during early adolescence, late adolescence, and adulthood. For example, both trajectories include the sampling years, which focus on letting children experiment with various ways of executing sport skills in various contexts through deliberate play and involvement for fun in several sports. The DMSP suggest that children should spend more time in deliberate play activities than in deliberate practice activities during the sampling years (age 6–12). However, as children age and mature, the recommended amount of deliberate play activities can be slowly replaced by deliberate practice activities, depending on the eventual goals of the individual (e.g. recreation or elite sport participation). Thus, in youth sport programs, the time component of the PPCT model should focus on how playing and training activities change throughout development, as outlined by the DMSP.

### Conclusion

This chapter has examined research in youth sport through an integrated developmental and ecological lens. The PPCT components of Bronfebrenner's ecological system theory and principles of positive youth development combined with the DMSP served as a framework to increase understanding of healthy youth development through sport participation. Based on youth sport research, particularly Côté and colleagues' DMSP, the following suggestions are made for youth sport programs aiming to promote positive youth development.

1   Sport programs for children (i.e. age 6–12) should include interactions between children, and between children and adults, that are based on play and opportunities to try out different forms of sporting activities. 'Sampling' and 'playing' during childhood are posited as the *proximal processes* that form the primary mechanism for continued sport participation at a recreational or elite level.

2   Sport programs during adolescence (i.e. age 13+) can change to include proximal processes built upon more specific training activities and specialization in one sport. As such, adolescents should have the opportunity to either choose to specialize in their favorite sport or continue in sport at a recreational level.

3   The developmental assets of the *person* (i.e. child or adolescent) involved in a sport program should be a priority of coaches, parents, and adults involved in the sport experience.

4   The eight setting features of the NRCIM should be implemented in sport programs to provide youth with a *context* that promotes developmental assets and the growth of life skills, competency, and responsibility.

5   Youth sport programs must be designed in consideration of children's healthy development over *time*. Administrators, coaches, and parents must look beyond the next game or the season final, to focus as well on the long-term positive developmental outcomes of the child-athlete.

6   The role of coaches and parents in sport is more than simply promoting motor skill development. Parents and coaches have a significant impact on the personal and social development of children involved in sport. Given the importance of these relationships, appropriate training that includes the principles of positive youth development should be provided to all adult leaders in youth sport programs.

The PPCT model serves to highlight the multiple features that should be combined to design and deliver youth sport programs that promote physical health, motor skill development, and psychosocial development. This chapter has showed that these three objectives are not mutually exclusive and that effectively designed sport programs can contribute to healthy youth development. In light of the role that sport can have on the whole development of youth, it becomes imperative that youth sport and positive youth development research inform each other on the best available means to promote enhanced life for all youth.

### Acknowledgements

Support for the writing of this chapter was given by the Social Sciences and Humanities Research Council of Canada (SSHRC Grants # 410-05-1949, .752-2005-1650, and 756-2006-022). The authors are grateful to Scott Wilkes for his helpful comments in the preparation of this chapter.

# References

Allen, J. B. (2003) 'Social motivation in youth sport', *Journal of Sport and Exercise Psychology*, 25: 551–67.

Benson, P. L. (1997) *All Kids are our Kids: What Communities Must Do to Raise Caring and Responsible Children and Adolescents*. San Francisco: Jossey-Bass.

Benson, P. L., Leffert, N., Scales, P. C., and Blyth, D. A. (1998) 'Beyond the "village" rhetoric: creating healthy communities for children and adolescents', *Applied Developmental Science*, 2: 138–59.

Black, S. J., and Weiss, M. R. (1992) 'The relationship among perceived coaching behaviors, perception of ability, and motivation in competitive age group swimmers', *Journal of Sport and Exercise Psychology*, 14: 309–25.

Bredemeier, B. J. (1995) 'Divergence in children's moral reasoning about issues in daily life and sport specific contexts', *International Journal of Sport Psychology*, 26: 453–63.

Bronfenbrenner, U. (1977) 'Toward an experimental ecology of human development', *American Psychologist*, 32: 513–31.

Bronfenbrenner, U. (1995) 'Developmental ecology through space and time: a future perspective', in P. Moen, G. H. Elder, Jr., and K. Lüscher (eds), *Examining Lives in Context: Perspectives on the Ecology of Human Development*. Washington, DC: American Psychological Association.

Bronfenbrenner, U. (1999) 'Environments in developmental perspective: theoretical and operational models', in S. L. Friedman and T. D. Wachs (eds), *Measuring Environment across the Life Span*, pp. 3–28. Washington, DC: American Psychological Association.

Brustad, R. J., Babkes, M. L., and Smith, A. L. (2001) 'Youth in sport: psychological considerations', in R. N. Singer, H. A. Hausenblas, and C. M. Janelle (eds), *Handbook of Sport Psychology* (2nd edn), pp. 604–35. New York: Wiley.

Carlson, R. C. (1988) 'The socialization of elite tennis players in Sweden: an analysis of the players' backgrounds and development', *Sociology of Sport Journal*, 5: 241–56.

Conroy, D. E., and Coatsworth, J. D. (2006) 'Coach training as a strategy for promoting youth social development', *The Sport Psychologist*, 20: 128–44.

Côté, J. (1999) 'The influence of the family in the development of talent in sports', *The Sport Psychologist*, 13: 395–417.

Côté, J. (2002) 'Coach and peer influence on children's development through sport', in J. M. Silva and D. E. Stevens (eds), *Psychological Foundations of Sport*, pp. 520–40. Boston: Allyn & Bacon.

Côté, J., and Fraser-Thomas, J. (2007) 'Youth involvement in sport', in P. Crocker (ed.), *Sport Psychology: A Canadian Perspective*, pp. 270–98. Toronto, ON: Pearson.

Côté, J., and Hay, J. (2002) 'Children's involvement in sport: a developmental perspective', in J. M. Silva and D. E. Stevens (eds), *Psychological Foundations of Sport*, pp. 484–502. Boston: Allyn & Bacon.

Côté, J., Baker, J., and Abernethy, B. (2003) 'From play to practice: a developmental framework for the acquisition of expertise in team sport', in J. Starkes and K. A. Ericsson (eds), *Recent Advances in Research on Sport Expertise*, pp. 89–114. Champaign, IL: Human Kinetics.

Côté, J, Baker, J., and Abernethy, B. (2007) 'Practice and play in the development of sport expertise', in R. Eklund and G. Tenenbaum (eds), *Handbook of Sport Psychology* (pp. 184–202, 3rd edn). Hoboken, NJ: Wiley.

Danish, S., Forneris, T., Hodge, K., and Heke, I. (2004) 'Enhancing youth development through sport', *World Leisure*, 3: 38–49.

Ericsson, K. A., Krampe, R. T., and Tesch-Römer, C. (1993) 'The role of deliberate practice in the acquisition of expert performance', *Psychological Review*, 100: 363–406.

Fraser-Thomas, J., Côté, J., and Deakin, J. (2005) 'Youth sport programs: an avenue to foster positive youth development', *Physical Education and Sport Pedagogy*, 10(1): 19–40.

García Bengoechea, E., and Johnson, G. M. (2001) 'Ecological systems theory and children's development in sport: toward a process–person–context–time research paradigm', *Avante*, 7: 20–31.

Gould, D. (1987) 'Understanding attrition in children's sport', in D. Gould and M. R. Weiss (eds), *Advances in Pediatric Sport Sciences: Behavioral Issues*, vol. 2, pp. 61–85. Champaign, IL: Human Kinetics.

Gould, D., and Carson, S. (2004) 'Fun and games? Myths surrounding the role of youth sports in developing Olympic champions', *Youth Studies Australia*, 23(1): 19–26.

Gould, D., Tuffey, S., Udry, E., and Loehr, J. (1996) 'Burnout in competitive junior tennis players: II. Qualitative analysis', *The Sport Psychologist*, 10: 341–66.

Health Canada (2004) *Young People in Canada: Their Health and Well-Being* (Health Behavior in School-Aged Children: World Health Organization Cross-National Survey). Ottawa: WHO.

Horn, T. S. (2004) 'Developmental perspectives on self-perceptions in children and adolescents', in M. R. Weiss (ed.), *Developmental Sport and Exercise Psychology: A Lifespan Perspective*, pp. 101–43. Morgantown, WV: Fitness Information Technology.

Jowett, S., and Timson-Katchis, M. (2005) 'Social networks in sport: parental influence on the coach–athlete relationship', *The Sport Psychologist*, 19: 267–87.

Lemyre, P., Roberts, G. C., and Ommundsen, Y. (2002) 'Achievement goal orientations, perceived ability, and sportspersonship in youth soccer', *Journal of Applied Sport Psychology*, 14: 120–36.

Mahoney, J. L., and Stattin, H. (2000) 'Leisure activities and adolescent antisocial behavior: the role of structure and social context', *Journal of Adolescence*, 23: 113–27.

Mallett, C. (2005) 'Self-determination theory: a case study of evidence-based coaching', *The Sport Psychologist*, 19: 417–29.

National Research Council and Institute of Medicine (2002) *Community Programs to Promote Youth Development*. Washington, DC: National Academy Press.

National Research Council and Institute of Medicine (2004) *Community Programs to Promote Youth Development* (Report Brief). Washington, DC: National Academy Press.

Ryan, R. M., and Deci, E. L. (2000) 'Self-determination theory and the facilitation of intrinsic motivation, social development, and well-being', *American Psychologist*, 55: 68–78.

Scales, P., and Leffert, N. (1999) *Developmental Assets: A Synthesis of the Scientific Research on Adolescent Development*. Minneapolis, MN: Search Institute.

Smoll, F. L., and Smith, R. E. (1996) *Children and Youth in Sport: A Biopsychosocial Perspective* (2nd edn). Boston: McGraw-Hill.

Tremblay, M. S., Katzmarzyk, P. T., and Willms, J. D. (2002) 'Temporal trends in overweight and obesity in Canada, 1981–1996', *International Journal of Obesity and Related Metabolic Disorders*, 26: 538–43.

Vallerand, R. J. (2001) 'A Hierarchical Model of Intrinsic and Extrinsic Motivation in Sport and Exercise', in G. C. Roberts (ed.), *Advances in Motivation in Sport and Exercise*, pp. 263–319. Champaign, IL: Human Kinetics.

Vallerand, R. J., and Rousseau, F. L. (2001) 'Intrinsic and extrinsic motivation in sport and exercise: a review using the hierarchical model of intrinsic and extrinsic motivation', in

R. N. Singer, H. A. Hausenblas, and C. M. Janelle (eds), *Handbook of Sport Psychology* (2nd edn), pp. 389–416. New York: Wiley.

Vazou, S., Ntoumanis, N., and Duda, J. L. (2006) 'Predicting young athletes' motivational indices as a function of their perceptions of the coach- and peer-created climate', *Psychology of Sport and Exercise*, 7: 215–33.

Wall, M. and Côté, J. (2007) 'Developmental activities that lead to drop out and investment in sport', *Physical Education and Sport Pedagogy*, 12: 77–87

Weiss, M. R., and Williams, L. (2004) 'The why of youth sport involvement: a developmental perspective on motivational processes', in M. R. Weiss (ed.), *Developmental Sport and Exercise Psychology: A Lifespan Perspective*, pp. 223–68. Morgantown, WV: Fitness Information Technology.

# Part II

# Instructional sport-based programs to promote positive youth development

# 4 Sport and responsible leadership among youth

*Don Hellison, Tom Martinek, and Dave Walsh*

## Introduction

The strength of adult–youth relationships account for a significant portion of youth program success (Rhodes 2004; Seligson and Stahl 2003). While acknowledging the importance of these relationships, the emerging field of youth development also emphasizes the need for specific program guidelines to promote holistic development among today's youth. The result has been a wide range of overlapping guidelines (e.g. Benson 1997; Brendtro *et al.* 2005; Lerner 2004; Noam *et al.* 2003), making it necessary for us to clarify our own youth development perspective in order to guide the development of a responsibility-based leadership program for youth.

## Youth Development in the United States

In the United States, the emerging field of youth development, with a jump start from a five million dollar study supported by the DeWitt Wallace-Reader's Digest Fund, has experienced enormous growth in the past few years. New journals have been started (e.g. *New Directions for Youth Development: Theory, Practice, and Research*), books and articles are being published with regularity (e.g. Halpern 2003), and programs of study have been developed at major universities (e.g. University of Minnesota, Michigan State University). Centers and institutes are also popping up here and there, including at Harvard University, a sign that youth development has 'arrived'. As is often the case, the practice of youth development has lagged behind these fast-paced conceptual and philosophical changes, although a number of exemplary youth development programs have been cited in the burgeoning literature (e.g. Hirsch 2005).

As the field continues to grow, more and more professionals, academics, and organizations are contributing to its conceptualization. Some focus on youth development programs whereas others emphasize the necessity of a community youth development plan. A sample of these contributions includes:

- The DeWitt Wallace Readers Digest study, *Strengthening the Youth Work Profession* (DeWitt Wallace-Readers Digest Fund 1996), pointed out the weaknesses of traditional youth work programs and identified key youth development program dimensions 'to foster self-direction, responsibility and empowerment' (p. 27) as well as psychosocial and competency outcomes.

- Peter Benson (1997) of the Search Institute promoted community youth development and described forty important internal (e.g. social competencies) and external (e.g. support) youth development assets.
- Hellison and Cutforth (1997), drawing primarily on the case studies of Milbrey McLaughlin and her associates (1994) and augmented by other studies and professional opinion, constructed eleven key criteria for state of the art 'inner city' youth development programs (e.g. strength-based, empowering, caring adult leadership, small youth groups sustained over time).
- The National Research Council (2002), led by a fifteen-member group of academics and professionals, 'evaluated and integrated the current science of adolescent health and development with research and findings related to program design, implementation, and evaluation of community programs for youth' (p. ix).
- Psychologist Richard Lerner (2004) offered a heavy theoretical-based approach to youth development practices and policies based on 'thriving and civic engagement' and promoted qualities of competence, character, connection, confidence, and caring/compassion.
- The High/Scope Foundation (Akiva 2005) recently released the New Youth Program Quality Assessment, a five-tier pyramid of youth development program principles in which only those programs highly rated by youth reached the top two tiers.

While these examples encompass a variety of interpretations of the emerging field of youth development, they do have much in common. All contrast markedly with the history of youth work programs (Halpern 2003) by embracing a holistic developmental perspective rather than 'keeping kids off the streets' or providing 'gym and swim' and other play-based programs. All three of the authors of this chapter, having attempted to provide holistic developmental programs for underserved youth without the support of the youth development movement, not only welcome but identify with this new field.

## Youth development and sport

Despite McLaughlin's (1994) inclusion of sport (basketball) in her youth development conceptualization, the physical activity field in the US has trailed most other areas in its advocacy and professional preparation programs for youth development. This is puzzling, because physical activity programs seem to be a 'natural' fit for youth development. As these are active, interactive, and highly emotional, opportunities for positive growth in conflict resolution, cooperation and team-building, goal-setting, and leadership abound. Instead, these programs are often viewed as 'hooks' to lure participants to after-school programs, rather than as programs beneficial to youth because of their youth development qualities (Hartmann 2003; Hirsch 2005).

Physical education has a rich history of arguing for 'education through the physical' (Siedentop 1990) – that is, using physical activity as a vehicle to promote whole child development. However, the integration of youth development goals and principles with physical activity programs has been slow to develop, both in practice and in courses of study offered by university physical education, kinesiology, and sport and exercise departments.

Fortunately, the field of physical activity is finding its voice (and conscience). Hudson (1997) made the connection to the allied fields of health education, physical education, recreation, and dance in 1997, followed by others, particularly Al Petitpas and his associates' groundbreaking prevention, intervention, and life skills framework for sport and youth development programs (Petitpas *et al.* 2005). Fraser-Thomas and her associates (2005) also linked sport with youth development, especially the youth development work of Benson, Lerner, and the National Research Council (all cited above). Physical activity-based centers and institutes have also been created, for example, the Youth Development through Sport Center at Springfield College (Massachusetts, US).

It should be noted that the field of recreation recognized the connection to youth development earlier than the field of physical activity, and has a number of related publications (e.g. Witt and Crompton 2002). Recreation includes physical activities as well as arts and crafts and other recreational endeavors, but a common assumption is that recreation is associated more with play than structured or semi-structured developmental experiences.

## Personal–social responsibility and youth development

Teaching Personal and Social Responsibility through physical activity (TPSR), a youth program framework based on a set of values and ideas, has a relatively long history (Hellison 1978, 1985, 2003) which predates the youth development movement. TPSR is closely associated with two youth development orientations, positive youth development and relational youth work (Edginton and Randall 2005), one of which emphasizes developmental stages and personal growth, while the other focuses on development through youth–youth worker relationships. TPSR is also associated with deCharms's (1976) early motivation work as well as Conrad and Hedin's (1981) social responsibility conceptualization, which consists of attitude (sense of responsibility), competence (ability to help), and efficacy (knowledge that one can make a difference). The most visible evidence of the linkages between TPSR and youth development is the recent book *Youth Development and Physical Activity* (Hellison *et al.* 2000).

In its current form, TPSR utilizes strong instructor–participant relationships based on specific guidelines and accompanied by gradual empowerment and group and self-reflection as tools to help youth take more personal responsibility – conceptualized as self-motivation and goal-setting – and social/moral responsibility – conceptualized as respect for others and helping others, as well as exploring transfer of these responsibilities to other aspects of their lives. Strategies have been developed to integrate these responsibilities into physical activity and to address problems such as conflicts that arise, and applications outside of physical activity are routinely discussed. TPSR also suggests five goals for program leaders as well as a daily format which provides daily opportunities to engage in group discussions and self-evaluation related to taking responsibility (Hellison 2003). These components are described in the appendix to this chapter.

The first author (Don) began to develop TPSR while teaching physical education to inner city youth in 1970 and later in alternative schools, detention centers, after-school programs. This fieldwork, which continues today, led to the development of a specific research strategy, service-bonded inquiry (Martinek and Hellison 1997; Martinek *et al.* 2004) and systematic studies of the impact of TPSR on youth. Some of these studies have been comparisons of responsibility-based youth programs to non-activity programs (Hellison and Wright 2003; Kahne *et al.* 2000; Walsh 2007), and a summary and analysis of twenty-six responsibility-based youth development program evaluations (Hellison and Walsh 2002). Other studies have looked at the influence of school culture and additional mentoring on the transfer of responsibility values from the gym to the classroom (Lee 2005; Martinek *et al.* 2001), factors affecting program commitment (Schilling 2001), and program effects on grades and office referrals (Martinek *et al.* 1999). Three centers of current TPSR are Project Effort at the University of North Carolina at Greensboro, the Responsible Youth Sport Project at the University of Illinois at Chicago, and the Urban Youth Development Project at San Francisco State University.

## Youth leadership

Youth leadership, as part of a more general advocacy for youth empowerment, has been cited in the TPSR literature (e.g. Martinek *et al.* 2006) as well as in several youth development publications (Benson 1997; Hellison and Cutforth 1997; McLaughlin *et al.* 1994; National Research Council 2002; Lerner 2004), and is sometimes singled out as a significant higher order youth development quality. For example, McLaughlin (2000) argued persuasively that youth leadership is a vital component of youth development whatever the content of the program (e.g. art, drama, sport). Peter Benson's (1990) research on capacity-building programs further highlights three important recommendations for those developing leadership programs for adolescent youth:

- Enhance social competencies, including friendship-making skills, caring skills, assertive and resistance skills.
- Emphasize the development of positive values, particularly those that engender a sense of social responsibility for the welfare of others.
- Place high priority on including opportunities that help others and allow for personal reflection on the meaning of help.

Over the years, we have seen evidence of the many positive contributions that young people can make to their community. One of these contributions is an inherent ability to lead others. By leading others we do not mean 'my way or the highway'. Rather, we see adolescents as capable of being caring and compassionate leaders. This type of leadership in turn becomes a two-way street where adolescent leaders then make caring and compassionate leaders out of others. The great payback is that it empowers others to be leaders in their own environment.

Unfortunately, the kids with whom we have worked have had few, if any, opportunities to act as leaders during their lifetime. Their school offers leadership experience to only a select few who have certain characteristics (i.e. they are inspirational, organized, intelligent, charismatic, assertive, confident). These leaders are traditionally classmates who are popular in mainstream peer groups. Therefore, the vision of leadership, especially for those who live in underserved communities like those we work with, is quite limited.

Our approach to youth leadership, therefore, embraces a model of leadership that includes *helping others* as one of its priorities. The model attempts to break the mold of traditional approaches to leadership development by having both moral intention and service to others as its cornerstones. *It is the type of leadership* that helps others confront the moral drama of life. *It is the type of leadership* that can be experienced in smaller areas of life like neighborhood sport clubs, schools, homes, soup kitchens, and churches. *It is the type of leadership* that can be acquired by all youth regardless of their station in life. *It is the type of leadership* inspired by Walter Percy's phrase 'we hand one another along' (Coles 2000). And, *it is the type of leadership* that requires kids to displace urges of self indulgence with those of spirited service to others. The kind of leaders we have in mind are those who lead by example, or hand others along the way, stir us, encourage us, and instill moral grounding for actions and words.

But, getting kids to be these kinds of leaders is no easy task. This is especially true for youngsters who have dealt with the challenges of social and economic neglect and an educational system that has marginalized them in many ways. Many of the ideas for helping youth realize leadership capabilities have come from our personal experiences as teachers in youth sport programs. Over the years these programs have provided values-based instruction for hundreds of underserved children who have struggled, academically and socially, in the traditional school settings.

One program headed by the second author (Tom) operates at the University of North Carolina at Greensboro (UNCG). The other is headed by the first author (Don) at the University of Illinois at Chicago (UIC). The program at UNCG is called the Youth Leader Corps. High school students who were previous members of an elementary and middle school TPSR-based sport club become members of the Youth Leader Corps. UIC's program is called the Cross-age Leadership Program. It also extends the sport experiences of participants who were previously involved in TPSR-based sport clubs. Both programs have been running for eight years. A third program, recently initiated by the third author (Dave), pairs university students with high school leadership candidates who, after training, then run TPSR-based programs for younger kids.

The intent of all three programs is to foster leadership qualities in these veteran club members. This is done by having the opportunity to teach the responsibility values to younger kids from various community agencies and programs (e.g. Boys and Girls Club, Head Start, National Youth Sport Program). Many youth leaders attend one of the local schools, while some are either in alternative schools or pursuing a General Education Development certificate. And, there are a few who have dropped out of school because of pregnancy or incarceration, but still attend the leadership programs.

### Preparing youth to be leaders

Preparing adolescents for leadership roles can be a very complex process. This is especially true when trying to transform dispositions of self-indulgence (which many of our kids have) to ones that are responsive to the needs of others. Enabling this transformation requires a clear understanding between what Heifeitz (see Heifeitz and Linsky 2002) calls *technical challenges* and *adaptive challenges*. According to Heifeitz technical challenges are those that we already know how to solve. Adaptive challenges are trickier because they have no clear solution and require a change in behavior and values (Klau 2006). Here are two applied examples to help clarify this distinction: Arranging transportation to bring younger children to program sites was a technical challenge for us; transforming them into caring compassionate leaders was an adaptive challenge. The distinction is important in that it allows us to understand what it takes to initiate and sustain the transformation from being a program member to being a program leader.

Formulating a set of pedagogical principles has also helped us prepare leaders to accept their leadership role and to advance them through various stages of development (to be discussed later). Informed from our previous fieldwork experiences (see Schilling *et al.* 2001; Hellison and Martinek 2006) as well as recent research (Heifeitz and Linsky 2002; Wheeler and Edlebeck 2006) we have found that different levels of empowerment need to be applied in order for adolescent youth to evolve into responsible leaders. These levels are:

- Level one: Provide leaders an open forum to share ideas.
- Level two: Give choices to leaders about program content, with whom to work, and how the program should run.
- Level three: Include peer teaching where decisions and actions affect fellow club members.
- Level four: Provide opportunities for cross-age teaching where they teach younger children sport skills and responsibility values.

There also is a fifth level of empowerment that requires youth to take control of their future. Experiencing this level will depend on how well youth can accept the responsibilities of empowerment at the other four levels. It will also depend on how we do as program leaders in providing the necessary guidance that will prepare them to be responsible contributors to their community.

## Evaluating leadership growth

Evaluation of our programs will continue to be a challenge. One challenge is the increasing pressure by funders (and sometimes our university colleagues) to align program measures with expectations of the public schools (i.e. grades, suspension rates, incidents of conflict). We are continually reminded of Robert Halpern's (2005) plea to avoid the pitfall of using irrelevant measures that are peripheral to the program's goals. Instead, our measures of program success have focused on broader developmental changes such as commitment, the kinds of leadership experiences kids are having, and attractors and detractors to leadership development.

For example, in the Chicago's Cross-age Leadership Program, attendance and perceptions of leadership growth by youth and adult program supervisors have been main focal points of the evaluation agenda (Cutforth and Puckett 1999). Data that were both quantitative and qualitative (i.e. interviews and field notes) showed that the youth leaders increased in confidence, concern for others, interpersonal and problem-solving skills, and enthusiasm in learning.

Schilling *et al.* (2007) examined interview data of veteran Youth Leader Corps members to see what factors impacted their commitment to be a youth leader. They found that program environment (e.g. opportunities for personal growth); program structure (e.g. program perks, role-related experiences), relationships (i.e. with specific individuals and in general), and personal circumstances (e.g. lack of alternatives, time investment) were critical attractors to program involvement. Program-related barriers included program logistics, program structure, and program relationships. Personal barriers included perceived alternatives, personal characteristics, and 'real-life' responsibilities.

In both programs, researchers have also identified various stages of leadership development through which leaders advanced (Martinek and Schilling 2003; Martinek and Ruiz 2005; Martinek *et al.* 2006). Similar to earlier evaluation studies, interviews, journal entries, and informal observations served as the major data sources. Based on moral and self-actualization developmental theories (e.g. Gilligan 1982; Kohlberg 1981; Maslow 1968), a stage framework was developed to see how youth progress in leadership. A continuum of leadership (four stages) was subsequently formed to show the emphasis that leaders placed on their leadership roles:

- Stage one: Personal needs.
- Stage two: Teaching skills.
- Stage three: Reciprocal learning.
- Stage four: Compassionate leadership.

Evaluation of the data also showed that movement across these stages was quite fluid. Personal struggles often caused considerable fluctuation among the four stages. Moreover, the stage framework helped to provide a type of 'measuring stick' for determining the leaders' progression throughout their participation in the program. By knowing where they were positioned, the program leaders could make the changes needed to move them along the stage continuum (Hellison and Martinek 2006).

### Beyond youth leadership

The third author (Walsh 2003; Martinek *et al.* 2004) recently conducted a study to explore the transition from youth leaders to exploring their career aspirations. To do this, he began by helping his participants think about coaching as a career, and then broadened this perspective to career exploration with emphasis on the 'procedural knowledge' needed to take appropriate steps toward fulfilling individual career aspirations. The experience of providing leadership for younger kids helped them gain insight into the meaning and purpose of such work. It also provided a realistic, hands-on approach to some of the difficulties of 'making it' in the real world and the need for problem-solving as well as organizational and verbal skills.

## Conclusion

In this chapter, we have argued for the importance of youth leadership within the context of youth development and sport. Although youth development has a number of conceptual frameworks, we developed the case for youth leadership based on one particular framework, TPSR, which has a long track record of practice and is accompanied by a more recent history of supportive research. In addition to offering a rationale for TPSR-based youth leadership within the youth development–sport context, we discussed strategies for preparing youth leaders and the evaluation of such programs. We trust that our ideas will serve as a starting point for those interested in starting their own program or those who wish to extend existing programs to new levels of youth development and leadership.

## References

Akiva, T. (2005) 'Turning training into results: The New Youth Program Quality Assessment', *High/Scope ReSource*, 24: 21–4.

Benson, P. (1990) *The Case for Peers*. Portland, OR: Northwest Regional Educational Laboratory.

Benson, P. L. (1997) *All Kids are Our Kids: What Communities Must Do to Raise Caring and Responsible Children and Youth*. San Francisco: Jossey-Bass.

Brendtro, L. K., Brokenleg, M., and Van Bockern, S. (2005) 'The circle of courage and positive psychology', *Reclaiming Children and Youth*, 14: 130–6.

Coles, R. (2000) *Lives of Moral Leadership*. New York: Random House.

Conrad, D., and Hedin, D. (1981) *Instruments and Scoring Guide of the Experiential Education Evaluation Project*. St. Paul, MN: Center for Youth Development and Research, University of Minnesota.

Cutforth, N., and Puckett, K. (1999) 'An investigation into the organization, challenges, and impact of an urban apprentice teacher program', *Urban Review*, 31: 153–72.

deCharms, R. (1976) *Enhancing Motivation: Change in the Classroom*. New York: Irvington.

DeWitt Wallace-Readers Digest Fund (1996) *Strengthening the Youth Work Profession: An Analysis and Lessons Learned from Grantmaking by the DeWitt Wallace-Reader's Digest Fund*. New York: DeWitt Wallace-Reader's Digest Fund.

Edginton, C. R., and Randall, S. W. (2005) 'Youth services: strategies for programming', *Journal of Physical Education, Recreation, and Dance*, 76(9): 19–24.

Fraser-Thomas, J., Côté, J., and Deakin, J. (2005) 'Youth sport programs: an avenue to foster positive youth development', *Physical Education and Sport Pedagogy*, 10: 19–40.

Gilligan, C. (1982) *In a Different Voice: Psychological Theory and Women's Development*. Cambridge, MA: Harvard University Press.

Halpern, R. (2003) *Making Play Work: The Promise of After-School Programs for Low Income Youth*. New York: Teachers College Press.

Halpern, R. (2005) 'The weak link between programs and academic impact', *Youth Today*, 14(5): 32.

Hartmann, D. (2003) 'Theorizing sport as social intervention: a view from the grassroots', *Quest*, 55: 118–40.

Heifeitz, R., and Linsky, M. (2002) *Leadership on the Line*. Cambridge, MA: Harvard Business School Press.

Hellison, D. (1978) *Beyond Balls and Bats: Alienated Youth in the Gym*. Washington, DC: American Alliance for Health, Physical Education, Recreation, and Dance.

Hellison, D. (1985) *Goals and Strategies for Physical Education*. Champaign, IL: Human Kinetics.

Hellison, D. (2003) *Teaching Responsibility through Physical Activity*. Champaign, IL: Human Kinetics.

Hellison, D., and Cutforth N. (1997) 'Extended day programs for urban children and youth: from theory to practice', in H. J. Walberg, O. Reyes, and R. P. Weissberg (eds), *Children and Youth: Interdisciplinary Perspectives*, pp. 223–49. Thousand Oaks, CA: Sage.

Hellison, D. and Martinek, T. (2006) 'Social and individual responsibility programs', in D.Kirk, F. Macdonald, and M. O'Sullivan (eds) *The Handbook of Physical Education*, pp. 610–26, London: Sage.

Hellison, D., and Walsh, D. (2002) 'Responsibility-based youth programs evaluation: investigating the investigations', *Quest*, 54: 292–307.

Hellison, D., and Wright, P. (2003) 'Retention in an urban extended day program: a process-based assessment', *Journal of Teaching in Physical Education*, 22: 369–81.

Hellison, D., Cutforth, N., Kallusky, J., Martinek, T., Parker, M., and Stiehl, J. (2000) *Youth Development and Physical Activity: Linking Universities and Communities*. Champaign, IL: Human Kinetics.

Hirsch, B. J. (2005) *A Place Called Home: After-School Programs for Urban Youth*. New York: Teachers College Press.

Hudson, S. D. (1997) 'Helping youth grow', *Journal of Physical Education, Recreation, and Dance*, 68: 16–17.

Kahne, J., Nagaoka, J., Brown, A., O'Brien, J., Quinn, T., and Thiede, K. (2000) 'School and after-school programs as contexts for youth development: a quantitative and qualitative assessment', in M. C. Wang, and W. L. Boyd (eds), *Improving Results for Children and Families: Linking Collaborative Services with School Reform Efforts*, pp. 121–52. Greenwich, CT: IAP.

Klau, M. (2006) 'Exploring youth leadership in theory and practice', in M. Klau, S. Boyd, and L. Luckow (eds), *Youth Leadership*. Special issue of *New Directions for Youth Development*, pp. 57–87. San Francisco: Jossey-Bass.

58    *D. Hellison, T. Martinek and D. Walsh*

Kohlberg, L. (1981) *The Philosophy of Moral Development*. New York: Harper Collins.

Lee, O. (2005) 'Navigating two cultures: an investigation of cultures of a responsibility-based physical activity program and school', unpublished doctoral dissertation, University of North Carolina at Greensboro.

Lerner, R. M. (2004) *Liberty: Thriving and Engagement among America's Youth*. Thousand Oaks, CA: Sage.

McLaughlin, M. W. (2000) *Community Counts*. Washington, DC: Public Education Network.

McLaughlin, M. W., Irby, M. A., and Langman, J. (1994) *Urban Sanctuaries: Neighborhood Organizations in the Lives and Futures of Inner-City Youth*. San Francisco: Jossey-Bass.

Martinek, T., and Hellison, D. (1997) 'Service-bonded inquiry: the road less traveled', *Journal of Teaching in Physical Education*, 17: 107–21.

Martinek, T., and Ruiz, L. (2005) 'Promoting positive youth development through a values-based sport program', *Revista Internacional de Ciencias del Deporte* (International Journal of Sport Science), 1(1): 1–13.

Martinek, T., and Schilling, T. (2003) 'Developing compassionate leadership in underserved youths', Journal of Physical Education, Recreation, and Dance, 74(5): 33–9.

Martinek, T., McLaughlin, D., and Schilling, T. (1999) 'Project effort: teaching responsibility beyond the gym', *Journal of Physical Education, Recreation, and Dance*, 70(6): 12–25.

Martinek, T., Schilling, T., and Johnson, D. (2001) 'Evaluation of a sport and mentoring program designed to foster personal and social responsibility in underserved youth', *Urban Review*, 33(1): 29–45.

Martinek, T., Hellison, D., and Walsh, D. (2004) 'Service-bonded inquiry revisited: a research model for the community-engaged professor', *Quest*, 56: 397–412.

Martinek, T., Schilling, T., and Hellison, D. (2006) 'The development of compassionate and caring leadership among adolescents', *Physical Education and Sport Pedagogy*, 11(2): 141–57.

Maslow, A. (1968) *Motivation and Personality* (2nd edn). New York: Harper Collins.

Metzler, M. W. (2005) *Instructional Models for Physical Education*. Scottsdale, AZ: Holcomb Hathaway.

National Research Council and Institute of Medicine (2002) *Community Programs to Promote Youth Development*. Washington, DC: National Academy Press.

Noam, G. G., Biancarosa, G., and Dechausay, N. (2003) *After-School Education: Approaches to an Emerging Field*. Cambridge, MA: Harvard University Press.

Petitpas, A. J., Cornelius, A. E., Van Raalte, J. L., and Jones, T. (2005) 'A framework for planning youth sport programs that foster psychosocial development', *The Sport Psychologist*, 19: 63–80.

Rhodes, J. E. (2004) 'The critical ingredient: caring youth-staff relationships in after school settings', *New Directions for Youth Development*, 101: 145–61.

Schilling, T. (2001) 'An investigation of commitment among participants in an extended-day physical activity program', *Research Quarterly for Exercise and Sport*, 72: 355–65.

Schilling, T., Martinek, T., and Tan, C. (2001) 'Fostering youth development through empowerment', in B. J. Lomdardo, T. J. Caravella-Nadeau, H. S. Castagno, and V. H. Mancini (eds), *Sport in the Twenty-First Century: Alternative for the New Millennium*, pp. 169–80. Boston: Pearson.

Schilling, T., Martinek, T., and Carson, S. (2007) 'Developmental processes among youth leaders in an after-school, responsibility-based sport program: antecedents and barriers to commitment', *Research Quarterly for Exercise and Sport*, 78: 48–56.

Seligson, M., and Stahl, P. (2003) *Bringing yourself to Work: A Guide to Successful Staff Development in After-School Programs.* New York: Teachers College Press.

Siedentop, D. (1990) *Introduction to Physical Education, Fitness, and Sport.* Mountain View, CA: Mayfield.

Walsh, D. S. (2003) 'Helping youth explore coaching as a possible future: a career club for underserved youth', unpublished doctoral dissertation, University of Illinois at Chicago.

Walsh, D. S. (2007) 'Supporting youth development outcomes: a mixed methodology evaluation of an extended day physical activity-based program', *The Physical Educator,* 64: 48–50.

Wheeler, W., and Edlebeck, C. (2006) 'Leading, earning and unleashing potential: youth leadership and civic engagement', in M. Klau, S. Boyd, and L. Luckow (eds), *Youth Leadership.* Special issue of *New Directions for Youth Development,* pp. 89–97. San Francisco: Jossey-Bass.

Witt, P. A., and Crompton, J. L. (2002) *Best Practices in Youth Development in Public Park and Recreation Settings.* Ashburn, PA: National Recreation and Park Association.

# Appendix

## Student goals: levels of responsibility

1  Self-control: respect for others' rights and feelings
   - Control temper and mouth.
   - Cooperate; include everyone.
   - Solve conflicts peacefully.
2  Self-motivation
   - Effort and persistence.
   - Redefine success.
3  Self-direction
   - Independence and on task.
   - Goal-setting and follow-up.
4  Helping others and leadership
   - Without rewards; because it is the right thing to do.
   - Helping everyone have a positive experience.
5  Transfer to other areas of life
   - Try these things out in other aspects of life to see if they work better than what you are now doing.
   - Be a role model for younger kids.

## Instructor goals

1  Develop 'kids first' relationships with youth
   - Recognize and respect individuality and individual strengths.
   - Listen to youth, ask their opinion, engage them in problem-solving.
   - Believe that, with practice, youth can make good decisions.
2  Integrate responsibility concepts and strategies with physical activity content

3   Gradually empower youth
4   Emphasize reflection
   • Self-evaluation.
   • Group problem-solving.
5   Promote transfer
   • One sentence reminders.
   • Ask for personal examples.

## Lesson format

1   Relational time
   • Check in with individual youth.
   • Give individual youth reminders or thanks for previous contributions to the program.
2   Awareness talk
   • Teach the levels of responsibility.
   • Ask for volunteers to tell everyone what the program is about.
3   Physical activity lesson
   • Integrated with responsibility concepts and strategies.
4   Group meeting
   • For youth to voice opinions and problem-solve.
5   Self-reflection time
   • Time to evaluate themselves in relation to the five responsibilities.

## Instructional strategies

1   Strategies for integrating each level into physical activity content.
2   Strategies to solve specific problems and situations.
   • Accountability strategies.
   • Conflict resolution strategies.
   • Strategies for problems that arise at each level.

# 5 Youth development through sport

## It's all about relationships

*Albert J. Petitpas, Allen Cornelius, and Judy Van Raalte*

## Introduction

The last decade has witnessed a significant increase in the number of youth programs that are based on the belief that sport participation can enhance personal development and eliminate problems, yet rates of delinquency, gang involvement, obesity, and teenage pregnancy have not declined (Biglan *et al.* 2004). Unfortunately, simply playing sports does not ensure that young people will learn the skills and develop the attitudes that will prepare them for productive futures. There is growing evidence, however, that if sport is structured in the right way and young people are surrounded by trained caring adult mentors, positive youth development is more likely to occur (Petitpas *et al.* 2004). This chapter begins with a brief description of a theoretically based and empirically supported framework for developing sport programs that can foster positive psychosocial development in youth. Two multi-site programs, Play It Smart and The First Tee, based on this framework, are presented. The remainder of the chapter focuses on strategies for training caring adult mentors, and a discussion of some of the training and supervision challenges that occur in large multi-site programs.

## A framework for positive youth development

This section provides a brief outline of the main components of a comprehensive framework for youth development through sport (Petitpas *et al.* 2005) which is based on the latest research and our own experiences with several multi-site programs. Based on this information, we believe that positive growth is most likely to occur when young people:

- are in an appropriate *context* for self-discovery (i.e. a voluntary activity that is intrinsically rewarding, contains clear rules and boundaries, and requires committed effort over time);
- are surrounded by *external assets*, including a positive community environment with caring adult mentors;
- learn or acquire *internal assets* that are important for dealing with various life challenges, and have opportunities to gain self-confidence by using these skills in leadership and community service roles outside of sport; and

- benefit from the findings of a comprehensive system of *evaluation and research* that identifies best practices and enhances service delivery.

This framework has provided a foundation for the development of several sport-based, multi-site youth development programs, including Play It Smart (football), Project Rebound (basketball), and The First Tee (golf). In Table 5.1, Play It Smart, a school-based team sport initiative operating in 136 high schools across the United States, and The First Tee, an individual sport, after-school program currently in 250 facilities in six countries, are compared in light of the specific elements within each of the four components of the framework. Although these programs address each of the elements of the framework somewhat differently, they both place primary emphasis on the training and supervision of the caring adult mentors who deliver the program to participating youth.

### Training mentors

The quality of the relationships established in both mentoring (Catalano *et al.* 2002) and counseling interactions (Sexton and Whiston 1994) has been shown to be instrumental in fostering adherence and positive outcomes for participants. In general, there is considerable support for the notion that youth development programs are only as effective as the adults that deliver them. Individuals who are not able to build trusting relationships with young people are less likely to create an environment where participants are willing to take risks and where they know that making mistakes is a normative part of the learning process. The developers of both Play It Smart and The First Tee recognized the importance of mentor training and have allocated considerable time and resources to ensure that participants have the benefit of caring adult mentors who understand youth development and who know how to build quality relationships.

### Play It Smart academic coach training

Although mentoring is a popular topic in the helping professions, there are few empirical studies that have examined the qualities of effective mentors. Recently, Cornelius (2006) identified three characteristics of academic coaches that correlate strongly with successful academic outcomes for Play It Smart participants. These characteristics are empathy, holding high and positive expectations for individuals, and advocacy. Based on this research, Play It Smart academic coaches are trained in the skills necessary to develop trusting relationships with participants, while holding them to high standards of performance. Academic coaches also learn how to demonstrate their caring by advocating for their student-athletes in a manner that does not foster dependency or feelings of entitlement.

The initial orientation and training for academic coaches working in the Play It Smart program happens during a week-long training institute that takes place prior to the start of the academic year. This training is conducted by the National Football Foundation Center for Youth Development through Sport at Springfield

Table 5.1 A framework for youth development through sport and two example programs

| Program elements | | Play It Smart | The First Tee |
|---|---|---|---|
| Context | Intrinsically motivating, requires commitment, provides challenge (flow) | Focus on high school football teams, with activities extending entire academic year | Focus on youth participating in golf program |
| | Valued place in a constructive group | Each participant is supported and guided in finding a special role within a valued group (Play It Smart) | Focus on self-improvements, opportunities to teach younger participants |
| | Voluntary, rules, constraints, goals, rewards and requires concerted effort over time | Play It Smart is an integral part of football program and has clear rules (e.g., mandatory study halls, attendance in classes), goals (e.g., team GPAs or hours of community service), and incentives (e.g., attend a college football game as reward for reaching academic goals), and involves participants throughout the entire school year | Voluntary after school program, golf has clear rules and etiquette associated with playing the game, life time sport |
| External assets | Close relationship with adult mentors | Academic Coach and Head Coach training and evaluation. Emphasis on assets and the quality of the AC/participant relationship | TFT Coaches and trained facility volunteers |
| | Involvement of parents and parental monitoring | Parent Booster Clubs, Parent Night programs, Parent Handbooks and Newsletters | Parent handbooks |
| | Structured activities that provide opportunities for participants to become external assets for others | Community service activities. Leadership conferences involving multiple Play It Smart schools | Becoming a "go-to person" is one of the core lessons in Eagle and ACE levels of programming |
| Internal assets | Development of planning, social, and problem solving skills | Focus on future planning, decision making, and problem-solving through team building and other one-on-one and group activities (e.g., ropes courses, college campus visits) | Clear core curriculum that addresses interpersonal, self-management, decision making, and resistance skills |

(continued ...)

Table 5.1 continued

| Program elements | | Play It Smart | The First Tee |
|---|---|---|---|
| | Sense of identity and purpose (hope and plan for the future) | Promotes identification with Play It Smart participants and supporters across the United States by creating learning teams (positive gangs) that fosters expectations for higher education and future careers | Career/life planning core lesson in eagle level and new career and academic planning emphasis in newly created ACE level |
| | Transfer of Life Skills to different domains by involvement in community service and giving back to the community | Community Service Activities (e.g., tutoring and coaching younger students, reading to the elderly and nursery school children, volunteering at soup kitchens). Leadership roles outside of sport. Transferable skills workshops | Each core lesson contains a "bridge to life" segment that addresses transfer of skills at home, school, and social events |
| Research and evaluation | Evaluation of changes in positive and negative behaviors | Assessment of GPA, SAT/ACT, graduation and college matriculation, and community service, as well as related psychosocial variables | Evaluation of participants knowledge of and ability to state how they used core lesson life skills in non-golf situations |
| | Evaluation of program effectiveness beyond the conclusion of the program or intervention | Follows each student throughout their high school years and beyond (e.g., Adjustment to College) by tracking their academic, personal, and career progression | Follow up evaluation of those individuals who earned college scholarships through TFT Scholars Program |
| | Assessment of which program components lead to positive developmental changes | Assesses which program components have the largest impact (e.g., quality of academic coach/participant relationship or various program activities) | Have begun a longitudinal investigation of several implementation variables and their effect on program outcomes |

College (NFFC@SC). Although most of the first year academic coaches have or are working toward advanced degrees in psychology, counseling, or education, all new academic coaches spend the first three days of training learning strategies to not only implement the program, but also how to gain entry into their specific school system and how to build relationships with all major stakeholder groups (i.e. student-athletes, coaches, school personal, parents, and local community leaders). Basic listening and counseling skills are reinforced through the Littlefoot approach (Petitpas 2000), and training participants have multiple opportunities to practice these skills under the supervision of the training team.

Veteran academic coaches join the new academic coaches for the last three days of the week-long training experience. During this time, all academic coaches are brought up to speed on the current status of Play It Smart, instructed on any changes to collegiate academic eligibility requirements (i.e. NCAA Clearinghouse) or achievement testing (i.e. SAT or ACT) that may have occurred during the last year, as well as trained in the latest strategies for study skills, crisis management, life–work planning, the use of incentives, and a wide range of other topics. New academic coaches also benefit from structured interactions with the veteran coaches on how to create experiences to facilitate attainment of the academic, career, life skills, and community service goals of the program. In addition, new and veteran academic coaches are provided with new materials, best practices, and marketing ideas through a program fair and information exchanges.

Following the summer training institute, academic coaches receive additional training and support in several ways. All academic coaches participate in regional meetings that take place during February. These meetings provide academic coaches with opportunities to network with peers and engage in a series of group problem-solving activities. For example, an academic coach would present a situation that happened as part of his or her program to a group of other academic coaches. The group would discuss the case, develop a list of strategies to address the issues discussed, anticipate the advantages and disadvantages of each strategy, and then decide on one approach to try to implement. This problem-solving methodology empowers academic coaches to take ownership for finding solutions to problem situations and strengthens regional support networks.

Academic coaches also receive educational materials and informational support from the professional staff at the NFFC@SC. Center staff members produce and disseminate workbooks on a variety of topics, including various life skills, academic and career planning, and learning strategies. Center staff members also provide supervision and consultation to academic coaches and regional coordinators. Finally, each academic coach works under the supervision of a regional coordinator or city manager who maintains regular contact and on-site consultations. The Promoting Academic Coach Excellence (PACE) program is used to identify and evaluate specific activities that should be carried out in support of the outcome goals established for Play It Smart.

*The First Tee coach training program*

The First Tee (TFT) Coach Program (The First Tee 2006) was created to ensure that individuals would learn how to deliver the life skills curriculum in a manner consistent with the framework for youth development that was presented earlier. After completing several prerequisite activities (e.g. reading TFT Life Skills Coach Guide), individuals participate in a series of three two- or three-day training experiences as they progress through TFT Coach-in-Training Phases 1–3. Training sessions are spaced out over a two-year period and trainees are required to complete several activities (e.g. develop and submit original lesson plans for core lessons, complete a telephone interview with TFT home office staff member) before they can progress to the next level of training.

To ensure that the curriculum is implemented in a relatively consistent manner across all sites, TFT developed a set of building blocks that serve as the cornerstones for the delivery of the life skill core lessons. The four building blocks are: a) activity-based; b) mastery-driven; c) empower youth; and d) continuous learning. The activity-based building block is based on the belief that a learning environment that emphasizes more 'doing versus telling' and introduces golf and life skills in a 'fun and seamless' fashion is likely to hold the interest of participants as they engage in self-discovery. The goal of a mastery-driven approach is to create an environment that focuses on self-improvements rather than social comparisons. As a result, TFT coaches strive to 'balance process and outcomes' by emphasizing the importance of paying attention to the specific behaviors (process) that are likely to lead to the individual's desired outcomes. For example, if a participant wants to make her high school golf team (outcome), she may recognize that maintaining balance (process) is a key to developing the effective golf swing she will need to meet her outcome goal. A TFT coach could assist the golfer by creating fun activities that focus on balance and could provide feedback on her ability to maintain balance (and not necessarily on the outcome of the specific shot). TFT refers to this strategy as 'intention equals attention'. Empower youth is the third building block and this segment of training focuses on helping TFT coaches learn strategies to remain 'youth centered' in their interactions by striving to understand participants' experiences from their perspectives. The belief is that, by using appropriate listening and relationship building skills, TFT coaches will empower youth and become mentors rather than simply instructors of the golf swing. The final building block is continuous learning, which provides a format for self-evaluation and for providing feedback to participants through 'coachable moments'.

The training of TFT coaches follows a developmental learning framework in which participants progress through three stages of understanding, namely exposure, application, and mastery. At phase 1, even though participants are exposed to the entire life skills core curriculum, TFT philosophy, and TFT coach building blocks, primary emphasis is placed on the par level core lessons and the activity-based building block. During the first day, TFT coaches in training participate in several core lessons as students and then have opportunities to provide feedback about their experiences. This format allows TFT home office staff to demonstrate the building blocks and model how to organize and implement the core lessons. The remainder of the first day is spent developing a par level core lesson plan under the direction of home office personnel. The second day of phase 1 training provides opportunities for TFT coaches in training to work directly with home office staff to deliver their core lesson to groups of boys and girls from the local area.

The goal of phase 2 of TFT coach program is to provide opportunities for TFT coaches to demonstrate their understanding of and ability to apply the building blocks. TFT home office staff take on less of a leadership role and allow TFT coaches in training to create and deliver birdie and eagle level core lessons. The primary focus of training and supervision during this phase shifts to developing activities that promote a mastery-driven learning environment that empowers youth. TFT coaches in training also have opportunities to deliver birdie and eagle level core lessons to groups of participants from the local TFT facility.

The third phase of TFT coach in training progression is conducted over a three-day period and emphasizes the continuing education building block. Coaches in training have opportunities to demonstrate their advanced understanding of the core curriculum through creating comprehensive lesson plans, delivering eagle level core lessons to area youth, and presenting information to their peers and to the home office staff in attendance. Although TFT coaches in training may not have attained 'mastery' of all the materials and delivery formats, they know the information well enough to incorporate their own ideas and activities into their lesson plans. In addition, considerable time is spent on a series of self-awareness activities and learning and demonstrating more advanced listening abilities.

Upon completion of the three phases of training, participants must complete a series of additional requirements at their home facilities before earning the status of a 'Recognized TFT Coach'. These requirements include activities such as completing a minimum of two years of TFT core lesson instruction, delivering all levels of core lessons, mentoring eagle level participants, and providing training to TFT volunteers and other interested adults. Once recognized TFT coach status is achieved, coaches must complete continuing education requirements to maintain their TFT coach status.

## Challenges and roadblocks

Although both Play It Smart and TFT have been successful in promoting positive youth development, there are considerable challenges inherent in operating large multi-site initiatives. This section of the chapter is focused on several of these challenges: consistency management; recruitment, retention, and training of service delivery personnel; and supervision.

One of the initial challenges in growing programs to multiple sites is consistency management. Similar to a franchise model in which hundreds of locally owned and operated facilities function under the umbrella of a central agency, consumers should be able to expect the same quality of product and service no matter which local site they frequent. At the same time, savvy franchise developers understand that different circumstances, personnel, or local ordinances are likely to prevent exact duplication of the original product or service across an entire network. Therefore, most franchise operations spend considerable resources in efforts to ensure the quality and reputation of their brand is maintained at each site.

Similarly, youth development programs, like TFT, that have expanded to hundreds of facilities spread out across several countries, recognize the importance of examining the service delivery framework to identify which components need to be present to ensure the fidelity of the original program. Both Play It Smart and TFT recognize that schools and local facilities are likely to have their own unique structures, resources, and limitations that dictate how a program can be implemented on a day-by-day basis. Nonetheless, these programs should also have operational components that are essential and that must be consistent across every facility or program site. To this end, TFT has developed the ZONE (Zeroing in On Network Excellence) and Play It Smart has created PACE as the central part of their consistency management plans. Both ZONE and PACE are used to monitor progress and provide local stakeholders with a form of quality assurance, and to assist local sites in program planning, evaluation, and recognition of accomplishments.

A second challenge confronting multi-site youth development programs is the recruitment, training, and retention of the caring adult mentors who are needed to implement the program. Many multi-site, not-for-profit organizations cannot afford to hire or compensate adequately sufficient numbers of qualified staff. As a result, these organizations typically rely on volunteers or part-time service providers. When this is the case, these programs are more likely to have high turnover rates and a greater disparity in the experience and skill sets of the individuals applying for the positions. In addition, program administrators must continue to be diligent when screening applicants, verifying information on their resumes, and conducting thorough background checks to guard against potential predators. To manage all these challenges, program administrators need to be proactive by building relationships with local colleges, community organizations, and civic groups in efforts to identify potential candidates. Training protocols need to be adjusted to address the widening disparity in the maturity and skill set of the service providers. Supervision needs to be strengthened and a system of non-monetary rewards and incentives should be put into place.

An additional challenge facing multi-site programs is supervision. With an increase in the number of sites and greater geographical dispersion, supervision can become a logistical quagmire. Adding to this dilemma are greater demands in monitoring the consistency management plans and more involvement in on-site supervision and continuing education required by the experience and skill set disparities discussed previously. Therefore, as a result of increased travel time and a larger scope of supervision responsibilities necessitated by expansion, program administrators need to budget significant increases in supervision expenses. Individuals selected to provide supervision need appropriate competencies and organizations should consider retaining seasoned professionals to provide meta-supervision and ongoing consultation to the supervisory staff. In addition, supervisors' case loads typically need to be lowered and greater emphasis placed on developing local crisis management plans and referral networks.

## Conclusion

Within this chapter, a framework for youth development through sport has been outlined and two multi-site programs that are based on this framework have been compared and contrasted. The information presented in Table 5.1 highlights the flexibility of the framework, as shown in how differently Play It Smart and TFT have operationalized the elements of the framework. Play It Smart is a school-based program, with a clear academic focus, and TFT is an after-school program with a more general life skills focus. The importance of a strong mentoring relationship with participants is evident in both programs, but the length and structure of the relationship differs greatly. There is also a clear emphasis on life skills in both programs, but TFT is more highly structured in how these skills are taught to participants. In addition, both programs are pursuing lines of research and evaluation to assess outcome goals and to better understand how the programs accomplish these goals.

*Table 5.2*  A comparison of Play It Smart and The First Tee

|  | *Play It Smart* | *The First Tee* |
| --- | --- | --- |
| Mentor characteristics | • Minimum bachelors degree<br>• Majority have graduate education in Counseling, Sport Psychology, or related fields | • No degree requirements<br>• PGA/LPGA golf professionals<br>• Educators<br>• Volunteers |
| Employment status | • Independent contractors<br>• Not employed by school<br>• External to system | • Employed by local TFT chapter<br>• Internal |
| Target group for program | • High School Football players | • Boys and girls aged 5 through 18 |
| Goals of program | • Academic, career, and personal development of participants | • Golf and specified life skills |
| Duration of training | • 6 day orientation and basic training<br>• 2 day winter training<br>• 2.5 day veteran training | • Level 1 = 2 days<br>• Level 2 = 2 days<br>• Level 3 = 3 days<br>• Continuing Education requirements |
| Training topic areas | • Gaining entry<br>• Relationship building skills (empathy, holding high expectations, advocacy)<br>• Academic skills (study halls, SAT/ACT prep)<br>• Life skills | • Teaching golf and life skills seamlessly<br>• Creating a mastery climate<br>• Relationship building skills |
| Supervision | • Regional Coordinator and on-site supervisor | • Regional Managers |

There are further differences between the two programs that are highlighted in Table 5.2. Who the mentors are, their employer, how they are trained, and how they are supervised are factors that vary between the programs. The stated goals of the program and who the program serves also differ greatly. Yet, with all these differences, at their core these two programs have consistent features – a context for growth, with external assets of caring adult mentors, who are focused on developing the internal assets of the participants, with the support of a sound evaluation and research program.

## References

Biglan, A, Brennan, P. A., Foster, S. L., and Holder, H.D. (2004) *Helping Adolescents at Risk: Prevention of Multiple Problem Behaviors*. New York: Guilford.

Catalano, R., Berglund, L., Ryan, J., Lonczak, H., and Hawkins, D. (2002) *Positive Youth Development in the United States: Research Findings on Evaluations of Positive Youth Development Programs*. Retrieved 2 Feb. 2002, from http://aspe.os.dhhs.gov/hsp/PositiveYouthDev99/index.html

Cornelius, A. E. (2006) 'Evaluating the mentor–protégé relationship', paper presented at '"Let's Play" – Life Enhancement through Sport: Promoting Lifeskills and Academics in Youth' conference, Springfield, MA.

Petitpas, A. J. (2000) 'The Littlefoot approach to learned resourcefulness: managing stress on and off the field', in M. Andersen (ed.), *Doing Sport Psychology: Process and Practice*, pp. 33–43. Champaign, IL: Human Kinetics.

Petitpas, A. J., Van Raalte, J. L., Cornelius, A., and Presbrey, J. (2004) 'A life skills development program for high school student-athletes', *Journal of Primary Prevention*, 24: 325–34.

Petitpas, A. J., Cornelius, A. E., Van Raalte, J. L., and Jones, T. (2005) 'A framework for planning youth sport programs that foster psychosocial development', *The Sport Psychologist*, 19: 63–80.

Sexton, T. L., and Whiston, S. C. (1994) 'The status of the counseling relationship: an empirical review, theoretical implications, and research directions', *The Counseling Psychologist*, 22: 6–78.

The First Tee (2006) *The First Tee Coach Program: Overview and Requirements* (3rd edn). St Augustine, FL: Author.

# 6 Enhancing life skills through sport for children and youth

*Christina Theokas, Steven Danish, Ken Hodge, Ihirangi Heke, and Tanya Forneris*

## Introduction

Participation in all types of sports is extremely high for American children and youth. Recent estimates are that 47 out of 52 million children participate in or have joined at least one sport program (Ewing and Seefeldt 2002). Data from the Before-and After-School Activities survey showed that children in kindergarten through eighth grade are most likely to participate in sports after school (27 percent), followed by religious activities (19 percent), and then by art activities (17 percent) (US Department of Education 2001). Similarly, 58 percent of children age 6–17 participated in sports activities in the National Survey of Children's Health (2003) (Blumberg *et al.* 2005). Not only are the percentages of youth participating in sports high, but the rates of participation are rising. For example, during the 2004–5 school year, approximately seven million high school students participated in athletic programs, up from 5.3 million in 1990 (Lopez and Moore 2006). These data suggest that sport is a major leisure activity for young people in the United States. As such, there is great potential for sport to contribute to the development of children.

It is important to note, however, that youth sports differ quite dramatically from individual activities (e.g. horseback riding) to team sports (e.g. football), with different skills sets and competencies (e.g. strength, speed, dexterity) needed to perform effectively. What is common though is that young people are engaged in a physical, structured activity with one or a group of adults who serve as coaches and mentors. Children voluntarily join sports programs for a variety of reasons including interest, fun, or to be with friends, and they consistently report higher levels of motivation and cognitive engagement in these activities, which contributes to a diverse array of personal and interpersonal developmental processes (Csikszentmihalyi and Larson 1984; Larson 2000).

One clear goal of sport involvement is the promotion of fitness and health through an active lifestyle (Smoll and Smith 2002). Research has shown that the goal to be fit and healthy is a significant predictor for children and adolescents' decision to participate in both sports and physical fitness activities (Perkins *et al.* 2004). However, it is also commonly believed that, through sports, children and adolescents learn values and skills that will serve them well as they prepare for the rest of their lives (Danish et al. 2003). 'Sports builds character' is a widespread belief in American culture (Fullinwider 2006). Supporting that common dictum, Lopez and Moore (2006) found that youth who participated in sports during high school were more likely to have volunteered, registered to vote, and followed the news closely as young adults age 18–25.

The purpose of this chapter is to describe the role sport can play in preparing youth to learn essential 'life lessons', to provide examples of several sport-based programs designed to achieve these goals, and to discuss the barriers to the design and implementation of these programs. Life skills can be acquired through sports participation; however, we take the perspective that being intentional and directly teaching life skills is more effective than assuming assimilation will occur or by using a lecture-oriented approach that is common in coaching. Although information is easy to disseminate through lectures to participants, it does not predictably produce the desired result. At best, information may augment other efforts as it describes *what* to do, but not *how* to do it. We believe that a better alternative is the teaching of skills of *how to* succeed in life and why such skills are important. Moreover, skills, whether directed toward enhancing athletic performance or success in life, are taught in the same way – through demonstration, modeling and practice (Danish and Hale 1981).

## What are life skills?

We define life skills as those skills that enable individuals to succeed in the different environments in which they live, such as school, home and in their neighborhoods and with their peer groups. Life skills can be behavioral (taking turns) or cognitive (making good decisions); interpersonal (communicating effectively) or intrapersonal (setting goals) (Danish et al. 1993). Involvement in sports, like other activities children engage in, can provide opportunities to develop competencies across multiple domains of functioning.

However, the benefits of participation in sport are not transmitted through mere participation in games. There is nothing about sport itself that is magical. Being on the field or the court does not by itself contribute to the positive development of children and the acquisition of critical life skills (Hodge and Danish 1999). Researchers who have studied the effects of participation in sport and leisure activities have found both positive and negative effects (Barber et al. 2001; Mahoney and Stattin 2000).

Understanding youth's experience in sports is probably most relevant to understanding how and why positive or negative effects are found. For example, Strean and Garcia Bengoechea (2001) concluded that it was the individual's experience of sport that determined whether participation was viewed as positive or negative; Mahoney and Stattin (2000) found that the structure and context of the activity was important in determining whether participation led to positive or negative outcomes.

Moreover, the ability to transfer skills learned in sports to other domains is perhaps the most crucial step in achieving the maximum outcome from participation in sports. Development of sports-based life skills programs is essential to this process. In the following section, we discuss two sport-based programs, designed by the authors, that are focused on facilitating positive youth development. The programs clearly outline a road map as to how best to teach the skills or what may be considered 'life lessons' to youth.

## Examples of sport-based life skills programs

### Sports United to Promote Education and Recreation (SUPER)

SUPER is a peer-led series of 18 modules taught like sports clinics (Danish 2002b). Participants are involved in three sets of activities: learning the physical skills related to a specific sport; learning life skills related to sports in general; and playing the sport. SUPER is patterned after the nationally known, award-winning Going for the Goal (GOAL) program (Danish 2002a). GOAL is the 1996 winner of the Lela Rowland Prevention Award given by the National Mental Health Association. It has also been honored by the US Department of Health and Human Services as part of its Freedom from Fear Campaign and received an honorable mention by the Points of Light Foundation.

A description of the 18 modules is in Table 6.1. Each module or workshop is about 30 minutes in length. For an extended discussion of the conceptual framework for SUPER, readers are referred to Danish *et al.* (1993, 1996). The SUPER program has been implemented in conjunction with several sports including basketball, soccer, golf, rugby, and volleyball.

Student-athletes are trained as leaders and coaches for younger youth and participate in a service learning course. An integral part of the training focuses on how to use the Sport Observation System (SOS). The SOS emphasizes *how* youth participate and not just on *how well* they perform. Understanding 'how' provides information on the mental skills participants have in dealing with coaching/ teaching and is likely to be indicative of how they will respond to other forms of instruction such as school and job training. The SOS is presented in Table 6.2. SUPER student-athlete leaders are asked to speak to the members of their team about what they observed. A 'life skills report card' is given to each participant at the end of the program. The report card provides feedback to the participants on the 'how' *and* 'how well' they have done.

Hodge *et al.* (2000) have applied the SUPER model in the development of the Rugby Advantage Program (RAP) in New Zealand. Danish and his colleagues (Danish 2001; Brunelle *et al.* in press) have applied the model to golf. The First Tee is a national golf and life skills enrichment academy for adolescents. Results from an evaluation of the First Tee program indicated that the program had a significant positive impact on adolescents' prosocial values and that the community service experience positively affected the adolescents' level of empathic concern and social responsibility.

Papacharisis *et al.* (2004) applied an abbreviated (eight-session) version of the SUPER program to soccer and volleyball with Greek schoolchildren, aged 10 to

*Table 6.1* Summary of SUPER program

| Workshop | Program Content |
| --- | --- |
| 1 | **Developing a Team**<br>The program and the peer leaders are introduced. Participants engage in several team-building activities designed to enhance communication and understand each other's strengths and weaknesses. |
| 2 | **Dare to Dream**<br>Participants learn about and discuss the importance of having dreams for the future. They then identify career/school and sport dreams they have for 10 years in the future. The peer leaders share some of their dreams. |
| 3 | **Setting Goals (Part 1)**<br>Participants learn the difference between dreams and goals and how to turn a dream into a goal. They identify people who support them in achieving their goals (Goal Keepers) and people who may prevent them from achieving their goals (Goal Busters). |
| 4 | **Setting Goals (Part 2)**<br>Participants learn the four characteristics of a reachable goal (positively stated, specific, important to the goal setter and under the goal setter's control). They practice distinguishing goals that are important to the goal setter and goals that are positively stated. |
| 5 | **Setting Goals (Part 3)**<br>Participants practice distinguishing goals that are specific from ones that are not specific and goals that are under their control from those that are not. |
| 6 | **Making Your Goal Reachable**<br>Participants apply the four characteristics of one reachable goal to their own goals. They set two six-week goals; one for sport and a personal goal. |
| 7 | **Making a Goal Ladder**<br>Participants learn the importance of developing plans to reach goals (called a Goal Ladder) and make plans to reach the two goals they have set. Making a ladder involves placing the goal at the top of the ladder and identifying six steps to reach their goal. |
| 8 | **Identifying and Overcoming Roadblocks to Reaching Goals**<br>Participants learn how different roadblocks (e.g. using drugs, getting into fights, lack of confidence) can prevent them from reaching their goals. They identify possible roadblocks and learn and practice a problem solving strategy called STAR to help them overcome the roadblocks. |
| 9 | **Seeking Help From Others**<br>Participants learn the importance of seeking social support when working on goals. They identify people in their lives, a Dream Team, who can provide doing and/or caring help to assist them in achieving their goals. |
| 10 | **Using Positive Self-Talk**<br>Participants learn the importance of identifying their self-talk, how to distinguish positive from negative self-talk and how to identify key positive self-talk statements related to their goals. They then practice making positive self-talk statements. |
| 11 | **Learning to Relax**<br>Participants learn the importance of relaxation to reduce tension and how to focus and breathe as a means to help them relax. |
| 12 | **Managing Emotions**<br>Participants learn that managing their emotions, both in sport and life, is learning to be smart. They learn and practice a procedure, the 4 R's (Replay, Relax, Redo, Ready), to help them play smart both inside and outside sport. |

(continued...)

*Table 6.1* continued

| Workshop | Program Content |
| --- | --- |
| 13 | **Developing a Healthy Lifestyle**<br>Participants develop an understanding of the importance of being healthy in all areas of their lives. They also learn how to make changes to insure they are living a healthy lifestyle and are asked to make a commitment to such a lifestyle. |
| 14 | **Appreciating Differences**<br>Participants identify differences among individuals in the group and determine which ones are important and which ones are insignificant in reaching goals. |
| 15 | **Having Confidence and Courage**<br>Participants understand the importance of believing in themselves and learn how to develop more self-confidence. |
| 16 | **Learning to Focus on Your Personal Performance**<br>Participants learn what it means to compete against oneself and understand that competing against oneself to attain personal excellence can enhance performance. |
| 17 | **Identifying and Building on Your Strengths**<br>Participants identify personal strengths and learn how to use the skills associated with these strengths and the skills learned in the program in other areas of their lives. |
| 18 | **Goal Setting for Life**<br>Participants learn that goal setting is a lifetime activity and they set two goals to attain over the next three months. One goal is school related; the other relates to home or community. They assess whether the goals meet the four characteristics of a reachable goal and develop a goal ladder for each goal. |

12. Two pre-test, post-test comparison group design evaluations were conducted. The first study involved 40 female volleyball players on two teams; the second study involved 32 male soccer players on two different teams. In each study, in addition to practice time, one team received the intervention and the other team did not. In both studies, measures included assessments of physical skills; knowledge of the SUPER program; and self-beliefs about their ability to set goals, to problem solve, and to think positively. The results of both studies indicated that students who received the intervention indicated higher self-beliefs for personal goal setting, problem-solving, and positive thinking than did those on the control teams. In addition, students in the intervention group demonstrated an increase in program knowledge and improvement in physical skills compared to students in the control condition.

## Hokowhitu program

Although the sport-based life skills program described above has been taught to individuals who live in New Zealand's dominant culture (see Hodge *et al.* 2000), a life skills program loosely based on the SUPER program has been developed by and for the indigenous population of that country as well. The Hokowhitu program (Heke 2001) is a sport-based intervention program designed by New Zealand Māori for New Zealand Māori. The program used Māori language and culture in

*Table 6.2* The sport observation system

| # | Question |
|---|---|
| 1 | How attentive are participants when given instructions or observing demonstration? |
| 2 | What happens when participants cannot perform an activity to their expectations? |
| 3 | Do participants initiate questions when they do not understand something, or do they wait for someone else to talk first? |
| 4 | Do participants initiate conversation with others, or do they wait for someone else to talk first? |
| 5 | How do participants respond when they have a good or a bad performance? |
| 6 | How do participants respond when others have a good or a bad performance? |
| 7 | How do participants respond when someone gives them praise or criticism? |
| 8 | Do participants give up when they don't do well, or do they persist? |
| 9 | Do participants compete or cooperate with teammates? |

the program development, implementation and evaluation. This approach was known as 'Kaupapa Māori Research' and appropriates Māori preferred learning and investigation styles.

Several contemporary sport-based programs have facilitated the development of sport outcomes among the Māori in New Zealand, but the Hokowhitu program sought to use sport to teach life skills such as decision-making, time management, task-related discipline, and goal setting. Since Māori, and adolescent Māori in particular, have historically had limited success academically, are over-represented in the untrained labor force, and have a very high incidence of drug and alcohol abuse (Durie 1998), the Hokowhitu program seemed overdue. In addition, health statistics indicated that Māori health was deteriorating at a rate higher than that of non-Māori (Te Puni Kōkiri 1995a, 1995b; Van Wissen et al. 1994).

At present, very little published material is available regarding teaching life skills through sport from an indigenous perspective. Some research had determined that intervention programs for adolescent Māori require a different approach, since mainstream programs based on non-Māori cultural paradigms are often ill suited to Māori people (Blair et al. 1996). For many Māori, sporting achievement is a source of widely accepted *mana* (pride) and social prestige (Best 1976). To take an area of natural strength and build a program around these attributes was a way to connect with the culture.

However, it is not just the design of the program that makes it unique; it is also its development. Māori were enlisted as active partners in producing a program that is relevant and valid within their community. As an indigenous approach to education and intervention, *Kaupapa Māori* signifies the need for any intervention with Māori to be initiated, determined, and validated in terms of the worldview of Māori.

In the Hokowhitu program it was very important that Māori ancestral ideologies and social imperatives were retained. In addition to using a Māori preferred learning approach, several important cultural concepts were adopted. They included: *He kanohi kitea* (meeting face to face rather than email or phone contact for organizing participation), *manaaki ki te tangata* (providing funding for travel to and from events including food and supervision for school age participants), *kaua e takahia te mana o te tangata* (ensuring appropriate respect for participants and the importance of obtaining informed consent), *kaua e mahaki* (sharing all information with participants so that the community is able to get direct benefit), and *Tuākana/Teina* (older students assisting younger students).

The Hokowhitu program involved ten two-hour workshops taught by eight *Tuākana*: year 12 (form 6) and year 13 (form 7) senior high school students aged between 16–18 years old (see Table 6.3 for a brief description of the ten workshops). Although the *Tuākana* benefited from being involved with the Hokowhitu program, the main recipients of the Hokowhitu program were 25 *Teina*: year 7 (form 1) and year 8 (form 2) junior students aged between 10 and 13 years old. The Hokowhitu program also recruited 'Lifeskill coaches', or *Kaiwhakawaiwai*, who were employed by the Raukawa Trust Board (RTB) to train the *Tuākana* in communication, group management, and the teaching skills necessary for running the Hokowhitu program. The *Kaiwhakawaiwai* remained on site while the Hokowhitu program was being taught, but the *Tuākana* were encouraged to teach independently of *Kaiwhakawaiwai* intervention.

Throughout the ten sessions, sport was used as the metaphor for teaching life skills. The workshops were all named using the Māori language with an English translation included. The importance of placing the Māori title first was to assist the *Teina* and *Tuākana* in recognizing the legitimacy of the Māori language.

The Hokowhitu program was conducted and evaluated at an intermediate school by the Ministry of Education of New Zealand. They concluded that the program benefited youth, largely due to using the preferred learning styles and protocols of Māori. Although the health and educational status of many Māori

*Table 6.3* Overview of the Hokowhitu Program

| Workshop # | Program Content |
|---|---|
| 1 | Awheawhe Tuatahi: Whakamanatia o Moemoea: How to Dream of Achieving. |
| 2 | Awheawhe Tuarua: Kohikohi whainga: How to Set Achievable Goals. |
| 3 | Awheawhe Tuatoru: Whakatauria o Whainga: Presentations by Local Sportspeople about How They Achieved Their Goals. |
| 4 | Awheawhe Tuawha: Mahi Whakatakataka Whainga: Goal Setting Practice. |
| 5 | Awheawhe Tuarima: Mahi Whakatauria he Arahanga Whainga: Making a Goal Ladder. |
| 6 | Awheawhe Tuaono: Ngā Tūtaki ki o Whainga: Roadblocks to Achieving Your Goals. |
| 7 | Awheawhe Tuawhitu: Whakatina o Tūtaki: Overcoming Your Roadblocks. |
| 8 | Awheawhe Tuawaru: Mahi Whakarite atu me Kohikohi Āwhina: Making Better Decisions and Seeking Help. |
| 9 | Awheawhe Tuaiwa: Turapa me Matapopore: Rebounding from Setbacks and Rewarding Your Successes. |
| 10 | Awheawhe Tekau: Nohoia: Celebration. |

remains in a critical state (Smith 1992), the Hokowhitu program was partially successful in facilitating positive changes in academic self-esteem for both the junior and senior participants. One senior teacher commented, 'I think the *Tuākana* are a lot more focused and they are asking me more questions about university training than they ever have.'

At completion of the Hokowhitu program, none of the participating junior students disliked school. Moreover, there were improvements in coping with negative pressure, developing positive attitudes regarding future outcomes and learning to cope with peer pressure. However, the Hokowhitu program improvements by the adolescent Māori in academic self-esteem, intrinsic motivation for schoolwork, career awareness, and drug and alcohol awareness remained the primary objectives for the project.

In sum, the aim of the Hokowhitu Program was to integrate both the life skills and *Kaupapa Māori* ideologies so that a sport-based, life skills intervention could be developed that would prove effective with adolescent Māori. Just as important, however, was the sense of self-determination that existed – Māori determining what is best for Māori and teaching a program that is consistent with Māori culture. This subtle difference of instituting a *Kaupapa Māori* approach has allowed Māori to learn new life skills while remaining in an environment that does not view Māori as a minority but as an equally valid and purposeful group.

## Ideal program implementation

Sports are by nature structured activities with certain rules of engagement and types of interactions between individuals. These do, of course, vary by sport. However, there is generally a coach/instructor or someone skilled in the sport who is 'in charge' and responsible for management of the activity. By nature, participants follow directions and are expected to execute the skills and competencies as needed. Within these standard features of sports, the key question is how should life skills training be integrated?

If the sports program is designed to help the adolescent learn both sport and life skills, what is learned in the athletic venue must be able to be transferred to non-sport settings. There are a number of strategies that can enhance the transfer. They include: (1) designing conditions to enhance transfer at the beginning of the activity; (2) creating similarities between the environment of the activity and the environment where the transfer is to occur; (3) providing opportunities to practice transfer during the activity; (4) providing opportunities to reflect on the experiences; (5) involving peers who have successfully completed the activity; (6) involving significant others in the learning process; and (7) providing follow-up experiences to reinforce learning (Gass 1985).

In the case of sport-based life skills programs, both sets of skills must be taught, not caught. There is nothing about a ball or a sport venue that teaches life skills. Combining sport participation with lectures about the dangers of alcohol and drugs, managing anger, and staying in school, given by well-known athletes, is also inadequate. First, being told what not to do is common fodder for youth and, although the messenger may be important to them, the message often has a limited impact. If messages are to be imparted, they need to focus on what has made the messenger successful, on and off the field – for example, their strength of character, steely determination, and deep desire to succeed regardless of the hardships and barriers placed in front of them.

Second, and perhaps more important, it is necessary to remember that adolescents are active individuals. Their life experiences suggest they learn best by doing rather than by talking. A Chinese proverb best describes the ideal teaching process: I listen – and forget, I see – and remember, I do – and understand.

The basic process for skill teaching is: name it, describe it, and give a rationale for its use; demonstrate the skill so correct and incorrect uses of the skill can be observed; and provide opportunities for extensive supervised practice of the skill with continuous feedback. When integrating life skills and sport skills, special considerations exist. It is beneficial to provide a seamless transition between the two, yet if a goal of the program is to promote transference from one setting to another, some separation of the activities is necessary. After trial and error, we have concluded that if the life skill instruction is given too separately from the sport instruction, the life skills would simply be ignored or easily forgotten. If the life skill instruction is fully integrated into the sport instruction, it would be hard for the youth to understand how the life skills could be applied outside of sport.

As a result of this, we developed the following instructional design. We teach the general concept of the skill first. As part of the instruction we emphasize that successful athletes need to improve both their 'below the neck' (physical skills) and 'above the neck' (mental skills) abilities. Further, we explain and provide examples through activities for how both physical and mental skills can be practiced and improved in sport settings and how the mental skills can be practiced and improved in non-sport settings. Opportunities are then made available to apply and practice the skill in the sport venue. We also have the participants apply the skill to other areas of their lives and help them develop a plan to practice the skill in these other domains. Finally, we have the participants report successes and failures in applying the skill in both contexts, both during the session and at the next session.

## Conclusion

This chapter has focused on how sports programs and activities can be a venue for life skills training. Sports are a very common activity for children and youth, so offer great potential for enhancing developmental outcomes in areas beyond physical skill development and athletic prowess. The point made here is that the effort must be intentional. Although participation is often linked with developmental benefits, mere participation does not confer benefits; the quality and implementation of sports programs are the likely causal mechanisms of enjoyment and development.

The integration and focus on life skills as part of sport involvement offers much potential. However, the relative paucity of programs on the mindset transition that would need to occur with participants, parents, and coaches is significant.

Sport is a well-established institution with well-developed mores and traditions that many will resist changing. Although sports are 'where the kids are', the maximum potential of activities to enhance life skills and encourage the transfer of skills to other settings needs continued work and development.

## References

Barber, B. L., Eccles, J. S., and Stone, M. (2001) 'Whatever happened to the jock, the brain, and the princess? Young adult pathways linked to adolescent activity involvement and social identity', *Journal of Adolescent Research*, 16: 429–55.

Best, E. (1976) *Games and Pastimes of the Māori*. Wellington: A. H. Shearer, Government Printer.

Blair, S., Heke, I. and Siata'ga, P. (1996) *Evaluation of Adventure Based Counselling*. Dunedin, NZ: Education Department, University of Otago.

Brunelle, J., Danish, S. J., and Forneris, M. S. (in press) 'The impact of a sport-based life skills program on adolescent prosocial values', *Applied Developmental Science*.

Csikszentmihalyi, M., and Larson, R. (1984) *Being Adolescent*. New York: Basic Books.

Danish, S. J. (2001) 'The First Tee: teaching youth to succeed in golf and life', in P. R. Thomas (ed.), *Optimizing Performance in Golf*, pp. 67–74. Brisbane, Australia: Australian Academic Press.

Danish, S. J. (2002a) *Going for the Goal: Leader Manual* (4th edn). Richmond, VA: Life Skills Associates.

Danish, S. J. (2002b) *SUPER (Sports United to Promote Education and Recreation) Program Leader Manual and Student Activity Book* (3rd edn). Richmond, VA: Life Skills Center, Virginia Commonwealth University.

Danish, S. J., and Hale, B. D. (1981) 'Toward an understanding of the practice of sport psychology', *Journal of Sport Psychology*, 3: 90–9.

Danish, S. J., Nellen, V., and Owens, S. (1996) 'Community-based life skills programs: using sports to teach life skills to adolescents', in J. L. Van Raalte and B. Brewer (eds), *Exploring Sport and Exercise Psychology*, pp. 205–25. Washington, DC: American Psychological Association.

Danish, S. J., Petitpas, A. J., and Hale, B. D. (1993) 'Life development intervention for athletes: life skills through sports', *The Counseling Psychologist*, 21: 352–85.

Danish, S. J., Taylor, T., and Fazio, R. (2003) 'Enhancing adolescent development through sport and leisure', in G.R. Adams and M. Berzonsky (eds), *Blackwell Handbook on Adolescence*, pp. 92–108. Malden, MA: Blackwell.

Durie, M. H. (1998) *Whaiora: Māori Health Development*. Auckland, NZ: Oxford University Press.

Ewing, M. E., and Seefeldt, V. (2002) 'Patterns of participation in American agency-sponsored youth sports', in F. L. Smoll and R. E. Smith (eds), *Children and Youth in Sport: A Biopsychosocial Perspective* (2nd edn), pp. 39–60. Dubuque, IA: Kendall/Hunt.

Fullinwider, R. (2006) *Sports, Youth and Character: A Critical Survey*. CIRCLE Working Paper 44. Baltimore, MD: CIRCLE.

Gass, M. (1985) 'Programming the transfer of learning in adventure education', *Journal of Experimental Education*, 8: 18–24.

Heke, I. (2001) 'The Hokowhitu Program: designing a sporting intervention to address alcohol and substance abuse in adolescent Māori', unpublished manuscript, University of Otago, Dunedin, New Zealand.

Hodge, K., and Danish, S. J. (1999) 'Promoting life skills for adolescent males through sport', in A. Horne and M. Kiselica (eds), *Handbook of Counseling Boys and Adolescent Males*, pp. 55–71. Thousand Oaks, CA: Sage.

Hodge, K., Heke, J.I., and McCarroll, N. (2000) 'The Rugby Advantage Program (RAP)', unpublished manuscript, University of Otago, Dunedin, New Zealand.

Larson, R. (2000) 'Towards a psychology of positive youth development', *American Psychologist*, 55: 170–83.

Lopez, M. H., and Moore, K. (2006) *Participation in Sports and Civic Engagement*. CIRCLE Fact Sheet. Baltimore, MD: CIRCLE.

Mahoney, J. L., and Stattin, H. (2000) 'Leisure activities and adolescent antisocial behavior: the role of structure and social context', *Journal Adolescence*, 23: 113–27.

Papacharisis, V., Goudas, M., Danish, S. J., and Theodorakis, Y. (2004) 'The effectiveness of teaching a life skills program in a school-based sport context', *Journal of Applied Sport Psychology*, 17: 247–54.

Perkins. D., Jacob, J., Barber, B. L., and Eccles, J. S. (2004) 'Childhood and adolescent sports participation as predictors of participation in sports and physical fitness activities during young adulthood', *Youth and Society*, 35: 495–520.

Smith, G. H. (1992) 'Tane-Nui-a Rangi's legacy ... Propping up the sky ... (Kaupapa Māori as resistance and intervention)', paper presented at NZARE/AARE joint conference Deakin University Australia.

Smoll, F. L., and Smith, R. E., eds (2002) *Children and Youth in Sport: A Biopsychological Perspective* (2nd edn). Dubuque, IA: Kendall/Hunt.

Strean, W. B. and Garcia Bengoechea, E. (2001) 'Fun in youth sport: Perspectives from coaches' conceptions and participants' experiences', paper presented at the Association for the Advancement of Applied Sport Psychology, Orlando, FL.

Te Puni Kokiri (1995a) *Health through the Marae: Nga tikanga hauora o nga marae*. Wellington, NZ: Te Puni Kokiri.

Te Puni Kokiri (1995b) *Omangia te oma roa: Māori Participation in Physical Leisure*. Wellington, NZ: Te Puni Kokiri.

Tuta, E. (1995) *The Māori Athletes Commission Strategic Plan*. Palmerston North, NZ: Massey University.

US Department of Education (2001) *Before- and After-School Activities Survey of the National Household Education Survey*. Retrieved 7 March 2006 from http://nces.ed.gov/nhes

Van Wissen, K., Williams, C., Siebers, R., and Maling, T. (1994) 'Māori Health Research', *New Zealand Medical Journal*, 107: 135–7.

# Part III

# Related contexts and issues

# 7 Youth sport and social inclusion

*Richard Bailey*

## Introduction

> We can reach far more people through sport than we can through political or educational programmes. In that way, sport is more powerful than politics. We have only just started to use its potential to build up this country. We must continue to do so. (Nelson Mandela, speaking to the footballer Lucas Radebe; cited in Hansard 2002)

Nelson Mandela's statement reflects a widely held view that sport can contribute in distinctive and far-reaching ways to important broad social outcomes (Bailey 2005; Burt 1998). But is it really the case? Can sport bring people from different backgrounds together and, in doing so, can it act as a force for social transformation and change? In the increasingly popular language of policy-makers and practitioners, can sport contribute to social inclusion? This chapter examines the theoretical and empirical bases of arguments for sport's role in the social inclusion agenda, offering an international perspective on an issue that underpins many of the bold claims and presumptions being made for the power of sport in society.

Advocacy groups have, for many years, offered the social case for sport (Doll-Tepper and Scoretz 2001). More recently, researchers have contributed reviews and analyses of the social benefits and outcomes of sport, beginning with Driver *et al.*'s (1991) report in the US. Subsequent studies have appeared in numerous countries, including Canada (e.g. Canadian Parks and Recreation Association 1997; Donnelly and Coakley 2002), New Zealand (e.g. Sullivan 1998), England (e.g. Long *et al.* 2002) and Scotland (e.g. Coalter *et al.* 2000).

Policy-makers, too, have started to embrace a wider role for sport. The Council of Europe's study of 'Diversity and Cohesion' is typical of recent claims made on behalf of sport:

> The role of sport in promoting social integration, in particular of young people, is widely recognized. Sport . . . is a recognized social phenomenon. Sports offer a common language and a platform for social democracy. [Sport] creates

conditions for political democracy and is instrumental to the development of democratic citizenship. Sport enhances the understanding and appreciation of cultural differences and it contributes to the fight against prejudices. Finally, sport plays its part to limit social exclusion of immigrant and minority groups.

(Niessen 2000: 14)

These are bold claims, and attribute to sport a distinctive role in the realization of broader political objectives. It is not surprising, then, that initiatives like the United Nations International Year of Sport and Physical Education in 2005 gathered endorsements from the governments of over 130 countries for its goal to use sport as a vehicle 'for promoting education, health, development and peace' and as a 'universal language [which] can help bridge social, religious, racial and gender divides' (United Nations 2005: 1).

The UK government of Tony Blair (1997–2007) has been among the most enthusiastic endorsers of a social agenda for sport, with one report (Department for Culture, Media and Sport 1999: 22) suggesting that sport (and the arts) can contribute to 'neighbourhood renewal by improving communities' and 'performance' on four key indicators – health, crime, employment and education. Similar statements have followed from politicians (such as the All-Party Select Committee on Culture, Media and Sport, May 1999, cited in Sport England 1999), government departments (Cabinet Office 2000; Social Exclusion Unit 2000), the sports councils (Sport Scotland 1999; Sport England 1999; Sports Council for Northern Ireland 2001; Sports Council for Wales 2001) and other agencies (e.g. Health Education Authority 1999; Local Government Association 2001). So convinced are they that sport, especially youth sport, can play a key role in social agenda that the Blair Government invested more than £1.7 billion in school and recreational sport provision and facilities (Department for Education and Skills 2002). Summarizing such claims, Sport England (1999) suggested that sport can make a contribution to this 'new policy agenda' by contributing to a wide range of positive social outcomes, including reduced youth crime, improved fitness and health, reduced truancy, improved attitudes to learning among young people and the provision of opportunities for 'active citizenship'.

The language used in many of these recent policy documents is noteworthy, as it marks a change on emphasis in claims for the social benefits of sport. Traditionally, advocates tended to stress what might be called 'pro-social' outcomes (Bailey 2005); that is, sport was claimed to develop *personal* qualities like teamwork, fair play and 'character', that help make the individual better able to operate in and contribute to society (Mangan 2000; Shields and Bredemeier 1995). More recently, however, language usage suggests a shift of focus from the individual to the community, or more accurately perhaps, policy-makers have tended to subsume traditional discourses of personal improvement through sport within wider notions of civic engagement and community regeneration (Jarvie 2003). In this way, sport has become conscripted into the service of 'fostering self-esteem, human agency and social equity . . . an important step toward strengthening and expanding civil society' (Harris 1998: 145). It is this change in focus, from the individual to community as the main unit of policy analysis (Jarvie 2003), that has led some to consider the contribution sport might make to the social inclusion agenda.

## Social inclusion

Social inclusion is an increasingly widely used term to summarize a range of issues concerning poverty, social injustices and inequality, issues that would appear to be universal and prevalent in all societies. The notion of its converse, social exclusion, first developed as a sociological concept in France, but its use has subsequently spread (Freiler 2001; Rodgers 1995). In recent times, the term has become increasingly used in connection with developing countries (Sayed 2002), where the discourse of exclusion 'provides a much more powerful frame' (Betts 2001: 2).

Social exclusion can take different forms, such as lack of access to power, knowledge, services, facilities, choice and opportunity. Some have argued that there may be conceptual difficulties with these sorts of interpretations of exclusion, since they confuse symptoms with causes (Long *et al.* 2002). Alternative definitions draw greater attention to the processes of exclusion rather than simply the product of exclusion: 'Social exclusion refers to the multiple and changing factors resulting in people being excluded from the normal exchanges, practices and rights of modern society' (Commission of the European Communities 1993: 1). According to this logic, measures taken to reduce indicators of exclusion, such as health, education, employment, will not necessarily succeed in promoting inclusion if they fail to address the processes of exclusion.

It might be countered that the language of social inclusion/exclusion is merely a new way of referring to existing concepts of poverty and inequality (Beall 2002), but most uses of these terms presume a broad shift from viewing social inclusion largely in economic terms to one which places more emphasis on people and the development of 'social capital' (Bailey 2005). According to this perspective, social inclusion and exclusion refer not just to states or situations, but also to processes by which individuals are included or excluded, and goes beyond the reallocation of resources, to stress power relations, agency, culture and social identify (De Haan 1998).

The notion of social capital has become increasingly established amongst both academics and policy-makers (Baron *et al.* 2000). Its emergence within theoretical debate can be traced to the writings of thinkers like Bourdieu (1997), Coleman (1988) and Putnam (2000). Whilst it would be misleading to ascribe any strong sense of unity to these writers' perspectives, there are some recurring themes. Generally speaking, the notion of social capital that emerges is concerned with the role of social networks and shared activities, and is closely linked with concepts of trust, community and civic engagement. In this approach, emphasis is placed on social processes and on ways to enhance the organizational capacities of communities. Stated slightly differently, a uniting theme for social capital theorists is that of 'social cohesion', or the potential for it, which is addressed through creating or strengthening the physical, social and cultural infrastructures of communities. Investment, when it occurs, can be made in programmes and processes that develop skills, confidence, self-organizational capacity and strengthen social networks (Putnam 2000). Bourdieu, in particular, provided an important contribution to debates surrounding social capital as he consistently saw it as a resource, or form of wealth, which yields power. As such, he reminds us that social capital operates within a process of power relationships which in many cases are not equal. The problem for society, according to this view, is how the power is utilized.

## Sport and social inclusion

Since sports participation provides a focus for social activity, an opportunity to make friends, develop networks and reduce social isolation, it seems well placed to support the development of social capital. A series of connected dimensions of social inclusion (Figure 7.1) can be extrapolated from the literature (e.g. Donnelly 1996; Freiler 2001) that offer a useful framework for considering sport's potential contribution to social inclusion/exclusion (Bailey 2005).

First, the *functional* dimension of social inclusion relates to the enhancement of knowledge, skills and understanding. Sport, it is claimed, provides opportunities for the development of valued capabilities and competencies, and the anecdotal evidence in favour of sport's contribution to inter-personal and intra-personal skills is persuasive (Bailey 2006). Discussion in this area has focused primarily on the social character of most sports (Martinek and Hellison 1997), and the hypothesis that the need for individuals to work collaboratively will encourage (or necessitate) the development of skills like trust (Priest 1998), empathy (Moore 2002), personal responsibility (Hellison 2003) and cooperation (Miller et al. 1997).

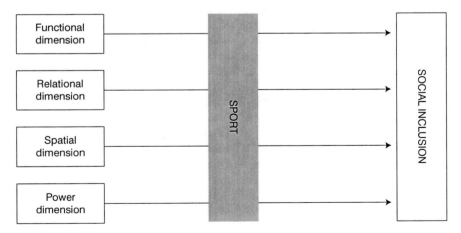

Figure 7.1 Social inclusion through sport?

The idea that sport provides appropriate settings for the promotion of young people's social development has led to the formation of a number of programmes aimed at using various forms of physical activity as vehicles for the development of valuable skills and capabilities (Cameron and MacDougall 2000; Morris *et al.* 2003; Sandford *et al.* 2006). It has also led to the development of a number of theory-based programmes, designed to teach young people personal and social skills, such as Siedentop's Sport Education approach (1994), Hellison's Personal and Social Responsibility model (2003) and Ennis's Sport for Peace curriculum (1999). Many of these programs and models have been evaluated, and their findings might be summarized as cautiously optimistic (Ennis 1999; Wright *et al.* 2004), with some of the most promising evidence coming from school-based initiatives, which have found that sport-based programmes can help improve student attendance, behaviour and attitude towards school (Sandford *et al.* 2006), as well as reduce young people's engagement in anti-social or criminal behaviour (Andrews and Andrews 2003; Cameron and MacDougall 2000).

Second, social inclusion can be defined in *relational* terms, such as a sense of social acceptance. Sport might play a role, here, by offering young people a sense of belonging, to a team, a club or community (Ennis 1999). Harris (1998) highlights the communal or 'civic' character of sport. Large numbers of people give a great deal of time to participate in sport, whether as a player, an organizer or a spectator. Players sometimes claim that sport can act as a point of shared interest bringing families together and encouraging people to interact in the broader community and beyond, often with people of different social backgrounds (Sport Canada 2005). Even young people who identify themselves explicitly as 'non-joiners' seem able to join like-minded peers in informal or 'lifestyle' sports (Wheaton 2004), and through this find 'a bridge between social and personal identities' (Chaney 1996: 134).

So, the relational contribution of sport to social inclusion is plausible. However, the relative absence of robust empirical data in support of such claims ought to remind us to remain rather tentative in our assertions. Moreover, the fact that to engage in most sports in developed countries costs money – for special clothing and equipment; for club membership and entrance fees for events; for insurance; and for travel (Collins 2004) – and many activities have become transactions provided by a large industry, suggests that much sport has become an act of consumption. And it is an act that is not equally open to all, since notions of normality/abnormality and domination/subordination seem magnified within the contexts of bodily practices: 'sport acts as a kind of badge of social exclusivity and cultural distinctiveness for the dominant classes . . . it articulates the fractional status distinctions that exist within the ranks of larger class groupings' (Sugden and Tomlinson 2000: 319).

Third, there is a *spatial* dimension, as social inclusion relates to proximity and the closing of social and economic distances. Certainly, there are frequent claims that sport brings individuals from a variety of social and economic backgrounds together in a shared interest in activities that are seen to be inherently valuable (Sport Canada 2005). This dimension of the social inclusion agenda lies, perhaps, at the heart of Mandela's enthusiastic endorsement of sport in his country's future, and a number of writers have suggested that sporting activities can act as distinctive tools for social integration and for 'nation-building' (Keim 2003). Drawing upon a theoretical framework first proposed by Harms (1982), Keim (2003) suggests specific ways in which such sport might support the development of spatial aspects of social inclusion. For example, there is a popular view that sport's non-verbal format can help overcome linguistic and cultural barriers more easily than other areas of social life. And the valued and socially prestigious character of sport could mean that people who might not otherwise meet come together for the sake of a shared passion.

Anecdotal evidence suggests that sport can bring people from different backgrounds together (Sport Canada 2005). Saunders and Sugden (1997) found that sport was one arena where cross-community interaction took place in Northern Ireland. Other studies have found that sport can also draw attention to divisions and differences (Sugden and Bairner 1993). At its best, then, sport can offer people and communities a meeting place (Keller et al. 1998), but, of course, sport does not always perform at its best.

Finally, social inclusion assumes a change in the locus of power. Sport contributes to social inclusion, in this respect, to the extent that it increases individuals' sense of control over their lives, as well as 'community capital' by extending social networks, increased community cohesion and civic pride. The establishment of social networks is a key feature of socially inclusive practices (Putnam 2000). This is especially important, it could be argued, within the context of sport for at-risk youth, for whom social and organized settings can be sources of anxiety or disaffection. Moreover, young people in general are normally seen as incapable of autonomous decision-making (hence the enforcement of compulsory schooling and protection, and the denial of the capability to give informed consent), despite findings that such self-determination is an important factor in supporting young people's engagement in social groups (Coakley and White 1992; Voyle 1989).

Some interesting data have emerged from studies of the sporting experiences of normally socially marginalized groups, such as women and minority ethnic groups. Deem (1986) argued, within the context of women in sport, that it can contribute to a more generalized feeling of empowerment. This is particularly important in environments where adolescents may be encouraged to view their bodies as sexual and reproductive resources, rather than sources of strength for themselves (Brady and Kahn 2002). Sporting activities may help young women develop a sense of ownership of their bodies and access the types of activity experiences traditionally enjoyed by boys (Thompson 1995). This may be because participation augments young people's self-esteem, or because being an athlete carries with it a strong public identity (Brady 1998). Some female athletes report having a stronger sense of identity and self-direction as a result of their engagement in sport – what Margaret Talbot calls 'being herself through sport' (Talbot 1989). Whatever the reasons, increasing the number of young people participating in sport does seem to open up routes through which they can acquire new community affiliations and begin to operate more openly and equally in community life. In doing so, young people's participation in sport can challenge and change social norms about their roles and capabilities.

## Towards socially inclusive sport

Evidence, to date, is limited with regard to the processes by which children and young people might become 'socially included' through sport, but there are some clues (see e.g. Donnelly and Coakley 2002). The research conducted to date has provided a rich source of information by way of the environmental and contextual factors that facilitate positive experiences for individuals within sport programmes, and consequently increase the potential for positive social impact. These include: having credible leadership of programmes (Martinek and Hellison 1997), involving young people in decision-making (Andrews and Andrews 2003; Voyle 1989), emphasizing the significance of social relationships (Shields and Bredemeier 1995) and ensuring an explicit focus on learning processes (Sandford et al. 2006). Coalter (2002) asserts that such examples of good practice are important for the development of future initiatives, and such sharing of knowledge would certainly seem to go some way to fulfilling the perceived obligation of educational research to answer the 'what works' questions (Slavin 2004).

Beyond these contextual factors, two dominant themes seem to emerge from both the theoretical and empirical literature regarding the necessary conditions from which socially inclusive sport might occur. The first theme is access. If sport is to be involved in the process of social inclusion, it is essential that children and young people have opportunities to participate. Evidence, to date, in this regard is far from encouraging. Research reviewed by Collins (2004) suggests that, in many countries, rather than including young people through sport, much practice actually *excludes* those for whom accidents of family and socio-economic background, education and geography create often insuperable barriers to participation. The centrality of such issues in this debate ought not be overlooked; without access, any discussion of social inclusion is moot.

There is also the issue of agency: arguably, inclusion is not possible unless institutions allow it to be so, hence the importance of projects that involve excluded young people in decision-making (Long et al. 2002). There is danger that centrally planned, administered and evaluated provision will be seen by would-be participants as either irrelevant or invasive. Generally speaking, sports programmes seem to be most successful when they have effective, preferably local, leadership (Coalter et al. 2000; Frisby et al. 1997), but the extent to which young people, who are usually seen as incapable of autonomous decision-making, can take part in genuine, equal discussions with adults is a matter of contention (Fielding 2001). Certainly, there are good reasons for policy-makers and organizers to at least listen to the views and opinions of those for whom their programmes are designed (Dyson 1995; MacPhail et al. 2003). As De Martelaer, De Knop, Van Heddegem and Theeboom (2000: 173), talking about their work in Belgium, state, 'Children are concerned about all aspects of their sport engagement ... Therefore they should be consulted in each new or existing initiative to be sure what adults organize for children meets the wishes and expectations of the target group.' But, there are contexts in which young people are capable of effective management of provision, as is evidenced by Voyle's (1989) work in New Zealand, which examined young people's management of sports facilities. She concludes that 'adult monopoly of power leaves adolescents with a choice between two alternatives: to comply with adult authority; or to choose not to participate' (p. 31). Of course, this is not a matter of absolutes: adult control *or* youth control. None of the studies of youth voice suggest that young people are uninterested in adult guidance and support. However, without strategies for negotiating and sharing power, significant roles and expectations, young people may find that the main choice confronting them is the way in which they will be excluded by sport.

## Conclusion

Donnelly (1993: 428) has commented that, 'We have long held, although with little evidence, that sport participation has the capacity to transform the character of individuals.' Whilst it is certainly the case that the enthusiasm sometimes expressed by advocates is not currently matched by the scientific evidence, it is fair to say that there is a sufficient mass of findings in favour of sport's capacity to contribute positively to young people's lives and their communities to offer some optimism. A case represents a possibility and there is certainly potential. Nevertheless, the futility of arguing whether sport is good or bad has also been observed by authors (e.g. Coalter 2001; Long and Sanderson 2001). Sport, like most activities, is not a priori good or bad, but has the potential of producing both positive and negative outcomes (Patriksson 1995). A more constructive question would seem to be 'what conditions are necessary for sport to have beneficial outcomes?' As indicated, above, we are starting to gather clues, but there is a need for further research.

A recent international review of the literature on outcomes of physical education and school sport concluded that these activities have the potential to make a significant contribution to the overall education and development of children and young people in many ways, but 'there is no reason to believe that simply including physical activities during the school day will necessarily bring about positive changes to children or to . . . systems' (Bailey and Dismore 2004: 7). In particular, the report suggests that the actions and interactions of coaches and teachers significantly influence the extent to which children and young people experience these positive aspects, and whether or not they realize the great potential of sport. Moreover, any effects will be determined by frequency and intensity of participation and the degree of adherence over time of the participants. These factors have been shown to be especially significant in the improvement of fitness and health (Corbin *et al.* 1994), and it seems reasonable to presume that they also have implications for the development of technical and social skills and particularly attitudes and values.

This chapter has sought to examine the plausibility and justification of claims for sport's contribution to social inclusion around the world. Despite the caveats and cautions expressed above, there is evidence in support of the claim that youth sport can contribute to the social inclusion of young people. As a relatively new area of research, further information is required before we can talk with confidence about the precise nature of this contribution, and it is especially important to examine the conditions under which sporting activities lead to positive outcomes. Nevertheless, initial findings are encouraging enough to warrant further inquiry.

# References

Andrews, J. P., and Andrews, G. J. (2003) 'Life in a secure unit: the rehabilitation of young people through the use of sport', *Social Science and Medicine*, 56: 531–50.

Bailey, R. P. (2005) 'Evaluating the relationship between physical education, sport and social inclusion', *Educational Review*, 57: 71–90.

Bailey, R. P. (2006) 'Physical education and sport in schools: a review of benefits and outcomes', *Journal of School Health*, 76: 397–401.

Bailey, R. P., and Dismore, H. C. (2004) 'Sport in education: project report', 4th International Conference of Ministers and Senior Officials Responsible for Physical Education and Sport (MINEPS IV), Athens, Greece, 6–8 Dec.

Baron, S., Field, J., and Schuller, T., eds (2000) *Social Capital: Critical Perspectives*. Oxford: Oxford University Press.

Beall, J. (2002) *Globalisation and Social Exclusion in Cities: Framing the Debate with Lessons from Africa and Asia*. Development Studies Institute working paper 01-27. London: London School of Economics.

Betts, J. (2001) *Unpacking the Discourses of Social Inclusion/Exclusion*. Uppingham: Uppingham Seminars.

Bourdieu, P. (1997) 'The forms of capital', in A. H. Halsey, H. Lauder, P. Brown, and A. Stuart Wells (eds), *Education: Culture, Economy, Society*, pp. 46–58. Oxford: Oxford University Press.

Brady, M. (1998) 'Laying the foundation for girls' healthy futures: can sports play a role?', *Studies in Family Planning*, 29(1): 79–82.

Brady, M., and Kahn, A. B. (2002) *Letting Girls Play: The Mathare Youth Sports Association's Football Program for Girls*. New York: Population Council.

Burt, J. J. (1998) 'The role of kinesiology in elevating modern society', *Quest*, 50: 80–95.

Cabinet Office (2000) *Report of Policy Action Team 12: Young People*. London: Stationery Office.

Cameron, M., and MacDougall, C. (2000) 'Crime prevention through sport and physical activity', *Trends and Issues in Crime and Criminal Justice*, 165. Retrieved 11 Nov. 2006 from http://www.aic.gov.au/publications/tandi/tandi165.html

Canadian Parks and Recreation Association (1997) *Benefits of Parks and Recreation*. Ottawa, ON: Canadian Parks and Recreation Association.

Chaney, D. (1996) *Lifestyles*. London: Routledge.

Coakley, J., and White, A. (1992) 'Making decisions: gender and sport participation among British adolescents', *Sociology of Sport Journal*, 9(1): 20–35.

Coalter, F. (2001) *Realising the Potential: The Case for Cultural Services – Sport*. London: Local Government Association.

Coalter, F. (2002) *The Social Role of Sport: Opportunities and Challenges*. Edinburgh: Centre for Leisure Research, University of Edinburgh.

Coalter, F., Allison, M., and Taylor, J. (2000) *The Role of Sport in Regenerating Deprived Urban Areas*. Edinburgh: Scottish Office Central Research Unit.

Coleman, J. (1988) 'Social capital in the creation of human capital', *American Journal of Sociology*, 94 (suppl.): S95–S120.

Collins, M. (2004) 'Sport, physical activity and social exclusion', *Journal of Sport Science*, 22: 727–40.

Commission of the European Communities (1993) *Background Report: Social Exclusion – Poverty and Other Social Problems in the European Community*. Luxembourg: Office for Official Publications of the European Communities.

Corbin, C., Pangrazi, R., and Welk, G. (1994) 'Toward an understanding of appropriate physical activity levels for youth', *Physical Activity and Fitness Research Digest*, 1: 1–8.

Deem, R. (1986) *All Work and No Play? The Sociology of Women and Leisure*. Milton Keynes: Open University Press.

De Haan, A. (1998) 'Social exclusion: an alternative concept for the study of deprivation?', *IDS Bulletin*, 29: 10.

De Martelaer, K., De Knop, P., Van Heddegem, L.V., and Theeboom, M. (2000) 'Organised sport: participation and experiences of children', in M. K. Chin, L. D. Hensley and Y. K. Liu (eds), *International Conference for Physical Educators: Innovation and Application of Physical Education and Sports Science in the New Millennium – An Asian-Pacific Perspective*, pp. 167–74. Hong Kong: Hong Kong Institute of Education.

Department for Culture, Media and Sport. (1999) *Policy Action Team 10: Report to the Social Exclusion Unit – Arts and Sport*. London: HMSO.

Department for Education and Skills (2002) *Learning through PE and Sport*. London: HMSO.

Doll-Tepper, G., and Scoretz, D., eds (2001) *World Summit on Physical Education*. Berlin: ICSSPE.

Donnelly, P. (1993) 'Democratization revisited: seven theses on the democratization of sport and active leisure', *Loisir et société*, 16(2): 413–34.

Donnelly, P. (1996) 'Approaches to social inequality in the sociology of sport', *Quest*, 48: 221–42.

Donnelly, P., and Coakley, J. (2002) *The Role of Recreation in Promoting Social Inclusion*. Retrieved 15 Nov. 2006 from http://www.ccsd.ca/subsites/ inclusion/bp/pd.htm

Driver, P., Brown, B., and Peterson, G. (1991) *Benefits of Leisure*. State College, PA: Venture.

Dyson, B. P. (1995) 'Students' voices in two alternative elementary physical education programs', *Journal of Teaching in Physical Education*, 14: 394–407.

Ennis, C. D. (1999) 'Creating a culturally relevant curriculum for disengaged girls', *Sport, Education and Society*, 4(1): 31–49.

Fielding, M. (2001) 'Beyond the rhetoric of student voice: new departures or new constraints in the transformation of 21st century schooling?', *Forum*, 43(2): 100–10.

Freiler, C. (2001) *What Needs to Change? Social Inclusion as a Focus of Well Being for Children, Families and Communities – A Draft Paper Concept*. Toronto, ON: Laidlaw Foundation.

Frisby, W., Crawford, S., and Dorer, T. (1997) 'Reflections on participatory action research: the case of low-income women accessing local physical activity services', *Journal of Sport Management*, 11(1): 8–28.

Hansard (2002) *House of Commons Commission Reports*, 13 Feb. 2002. London: United Kingdom Parliament.

Harms, H. (1982) 'Die soziale Zeitbombe ist noch längst nicht entschärft, zur möglichen Funktion des Sports bei der Integration der ausländischen Arbeitnehmer und ihrer Familien', *Olympische Jugend*, 12: 6–7.

Harris, J. (1998) 'Civil society, physical activity, and the involvement of sport sociologists in the preparation of physical activity professionals', *Sociology of Sport Journal*, 15: 138–53.

Health Education Authority (1999) *Physical Activity and Inequalities*. London: Health Education Authority.

Hellison, D. (2003) *Teaching Responsibility through Physical Activity* (2nd edn). Champaign, IL: Human Kinetics.

Jarvie, G. (2003) 'Communitarianism, sport and social capital: neighbourhood insights in Scottish Sport', *International Review for the Sociology of Sport*, 38(2): 139–53.

Keim, M. (2003) *Nation Building at Play: Sport as a Tool for Social Integration in Post-Apartheid South Africa*. Aachen, Germany: Meyer and Meyer Sport.

Keller, H., Lamprocht, M., and Stamm, H. (1998) *Social Cohesion through Sport*. Strasbourg, France: Council of Europe.

Local Government Association (2001) *The Value of Parks and Open Spaces: Social Inclusion and Regeneration*. London: Local Government Association.

Long, L., and Sanderson, I. (2001) 'The social benefits of sport: where's the proof?', in C. Gratton and I. Henry (eds), *Sport in the City*, pp. 187–203. London: Routledge.

Long, J., Welsh, M., Bramham, P., Butterfield, J., Hylton, K., and Lloyd, E. (2002) *Count Me In: The Dimensions of Social Inclusion through Culture and Sport*. London: Department of Culture, Media and Sport.

MacPhail, A., Kirk, D., and Eley, D. (2003) 'Listening to young people's voices: youth sports leaders' advice on facilitating participation in sport', *European Physical Education Review*, 9(1): 57–73.

Mangan, J. A. (2000) *Athleticism in the Victorian and Edwardian Public School: The Emergence and Consolidation of an Educational Ideology* (3rd edn). London: Frank Cass.

Martinek, T. J., and Hellison, D. R. (1997) 'Fostering resiliency in underserved youth through physical activity', *Quest*, 49: 34–49.

Miller, S. C., Bredemeier, B. J. L., and Shields, D. L. L. (1997) 'Sociomoral education through physical education with at-risk children', *Quest*, 49: 114–29.

Moore, G. (2002) 'In our hands: the future is in the hands of those who give our young people hope and reason to live', *British Journal of Teaching in Physical Education*, 33(2): 26–7.

Morris, L., Sallybanks, J., Willis, K., and Makkai, T. (2003) *Sport, Physical Activity and Antisocial Behaviour in Youth, Trends and Issues in Crime and Criminal Justice*, 249. Canberra: Australian Institute of Criminology.

Niessen, J. (2000) *Diversity and Cohesion: New Challenges for the Integration of Immigrants and Minorities*. Strasbourg, France: Council of Europe Publishing.

Patriksson, G. (1995) 'The significance of sport for society: health, socialisation, economy – a scientific review', prepared for the 8th Conference of European Ministers responsible for Sport, Lisbon, 17–18 May 1995. Strasbourg, France: Council of Europe Press.

Priest, S. (1998) 'Physical challenge and the development of trust through corporate adventure training', *Journal of Experiential Learning*, 21: 31–4.

Putnam, R. D. (2000) *Bowling Alone*. New York: Touchstone.

Rodgers, G. (1995) 'What is special about social exclusion?', in G. Rodgers, C. Gore, and J. Figueiredo (eds), *Social Exclusion: Rhetoric, Reality, Responses*, pp. 43–56. Geneva: International Institute for Labour Studies.

Sandford, R. A., Armour, K. M., and Warmington, P. C. (2006) 'Re-engaging disaffected youth through physical activity programmes', *British Educational Research Journal*, 3: 251–71.

Saunders, E., and Sugden, J. (1997) 'Sport and community relations in Northern Ireland', *Managing Leisure*, 2(1): 39–54.

Sayed, Y. (2002) *Exclusion and Inclusion in the South with Reference to Education: A Review of the Literature*. Discussion Paper No. 1. Falmer, UK: Institute of Development Studies.

Shields, D. L., and Bredemeier, B. J. (1995) *Character Development and Physical Activity*. Champaign, IL: Human Kinetics.

Siedentop, D., ed. (1994) *Sport Education: Quality Physical Education through Positive Sport Experiences*. Champaign, IL: Human Kinetics.

Slavin, R. E. (2004) 'Education research can and must address the "what works" questions', *Educational Researcher*, 33: 27–8.

Social Exclusion Unit (2000) *National Strategy for Neighbourhood Renewal: A Framework for Consultation*. London: Cabinet Office.

Sport Canada (2005) *Strengthening Canada: The Socio-Economic Benefits of Sport Participation in Canada*. Gatineau, QB: Sport Canada.

Sport England (1999) *The Value of Sport*. London: Sport England.

Sport Scotland (1999) *Youth Sport in Scotland: Young People and Sport*. Edinburgh: Sport Scotland.

Sports Council for Northern Ireland (2001) *Sport for Young People in Northern Ireland*. Belfast: Sports Council for Northern Ireland.

Sports Council for Wales (2001) *Young People First: A Strategy for Welsh Sport*. Cardiff: Sports Council for Wales.

Sugden, J., and Bairner, J. (1993) *Sport, Sectarianism and Society in a Divided Ireland*. Leicester: Leicester University Press.

Sugden, J. and Tomlinson, A. (2000) 'Theorizing sport, social class and status', in J. Coakley and E. Dunning (eds) *Handbook of Sport Studies*, pp. 309–21. London: Sage.

Sullivan, C. (1998) *The Growing Business of Sport and Leisure*. Wellington, NZ: Hillary Commission.

Talbot, M. (1989) 'Being herself through sport', in J. Long (ed.), *Leisure, Health and Well Being*. Eastbourne: Leisure Studies Association.

Thompson, S. (1995) *Going All the Way: Teenage Girls' Tales of Sex, Romance, and Pregnancy*. New York: Hill & Wang.

United Nations (2005) *Sport to Promote Education, Health, Development and Peace*. Vienna: United Nations Information Service.

Voyle, J. (1989) 'Adolescent administration of a leisure centre: lessons for sports organizations', *New Zealand Journal of Sports Medicine*, 17(2): 31–4.

Wheaton, B. (2004) *Understanding Lifestyle Sports: Consumption, Identity and Difference*. London: Routledge.

Wright, P. M., White, K., and Gaebler-Spira, D. (2004) 'Exploring the relevance of the personal and social responsibility model in adapted physical activity: a collective case study', *Journal of Teaching in Physical Education*, 23: 71–87.

# 8 Physical activity and personal/social development for disaffected youth in the UK

## In search of evidence

*Rachel A. Sandford, Kathleen M. Armour and Rebecca Duncombe*

## Introduction

The so-called 'problem' of youth disaffection has formed the basis of much recent debate in the UK, and this has resulted in something of a moral panic concerning the threat that young people pose to social and moral order (Davies 2005). Such panics are not new, however, nor are they confined to the UK; indeed, Smink (2000: p. ix) describes youth disaffection as 'a worldwide problem'. Furthermore, understandings of 'youth in trouble' or 'youth as trouble', fuelled tendentiously by media representations of youth issues, behaviors and practices in contemporary Western society (e.g. unemployment, crime, underage sex, and alcohol or drug abuse) serve to reinforce and reproduce the popular narrative concerning youth disaffection.

The concept of disaffection is, however, rather loosely defined. Certainly, in the UK, the notion has been appropriated by social policy-makers and employed alongside a raft of overlapping terms, such as 'social exclusion', 'social marginalization', 'disenfranchisement' and 'the underclass', to describe groups of individuals who lack access to a range of desirable social resources and benefits (Sandford *et al.* 2006). In discussions about the experiences of children and young people, in particular, terms such as 'at-risk' and 'disengaged' have gained increasing currency in the UK (Department of Social Security 1999; Social Exclusion Unit 2000). Throughout this discussion, the terms 'disaffected' and 'disengaged' are used interchangeably to describe the groups of young people involved in the two projects under discussion. However, it should be noted that these concepts do not relate to a homogeneous condition, but rather to a cluster of behaviors, attitudes and experiences.

Alarm about youth disaffection is also manifest within the school context, where it is characterized by increased levels of disruptive behavior, truancy and exclusions (active disaffection) and low academic achievement, non-participation and alienation (passive disaffection) (Department for Education and Skills 2003a, b). This has led to a belief that something needs to be done to help young people learn how to behave acceptably, responsibly and, consequently, successfully within society. As Steer (2000: 1) noted, 'the problem of "youth disaffection" is increasingly occupying the minds of policy makers'. Action taken has included the development of school-wide behavior management policies (Pierce and Hillman 1998) and a plethora of intervention programs designed to re-engage 'disaffected' or 'disengaged' young people (Long *et al.* 2002). Such remedial programs tend to have broad aims that are focused around reducing deviant behavior, raising aspirations and promoting positive social development (Merton and Parrott 1999), and within this broad framework there is an enduring belief in the value of physical activity programs to secure a wide range of benefits for disaffected or disengaged young people (Sandford *et al.* 2006). Indeed, physical activity as a solution to the ills of youth has gained increasing support within policy discussions in recent years. For example, the UK Secretary of State for Culture, Media and Sport, Tessa Jowell, suggested that 'a good sport policy is also a good education policy, a good health policy and a good anti-crime policy' (http://www.uksport. gov.uk/template.asp?id=1581).

In addition to remedial programs, there is growing recognition that physical education and school sport provide appropriate settings for promoting young people's personal and social development (Hellison *et al.* 2000; Larson and Silverman 2005). In response to this, a number of public and privately sponsored initiatives aimed at promoting personal and social development for disaffected or disadvantaged young people are being created, and the projects outlined within this chapter are two examples from the UK. In each case, it could be argued that these initiatives are influenced by the 'social problems industry' (Pitter and Andrews 1997: 85) that has built up around the notion that physical education/ sport can address wider social concerns. However, while aspirations for the benefits of youth physical activity programs are extravagant, robust empirical evidence to support them is comparatively sparse (Long and Sanderson 2001; Morris *et al.* 2003). Therefore, although there is a strong theoretical foundation underpinning the field (e.g. Burt 1998; Hellison 1995; Lawson 1999) there remains a need for more longitudinal and systematic evaluation research that can build on this and provide detailed empirical evidence for the mechanisms by which change (allegedly) occurs (Bailey 2005).

## Description of specific programs

### Project 1: YST/BSkyB Living for Sport project

Living for Sport (LfS) is a behavior improvement project intended for young people who are having difficulties with one or more aspects of school life, resulting in active, passive or potential disaffection. The program is run by the Youth Sport Trust (YST) and funded by BSkyB as part of its corporate responsibility portfolio, and takes the form of a specific intervention that uses physical activity to re-engage a target group of selected young people. Launched as a 'pilot' scheme in January 2003, LfS entered its fourth year in September 2006, and now involves approximately 310 schools in England, Scotland and Northern Ireland. In the words of the YST, LfS 'recognizes that sport can create a spirit of adventure and creativity, inspiring 11 to 16 year olds and helping to improve attitude and behavior' while also helping schools meet their behavior improvement targets (http://www. youthsporttrust.org/subpage/living-for-sport/index.html). Schools apply to take part in the LfS project, and then receive a small sum of money to help them cover the costs of their chosen intervention. Within the project, pupils often work with their teachers and support staff (e.g. teaching assistants) to identify particular activities in which to engage, and also to set personal targets and goals. Pupils also work towards organizing a final sport event (often, although not exclusively, for younger pupils) and are rewarded at the end of the project with a celebration event (e.g. an opportunity to try a new activity or an awards ceremony). Most schools that undertake LfS serve areas of high social and economic deprivation, and many of the young people face challenging personal and social circumstances.

### Project 2: HSBC/Outward Bound partnership project

The HSBC/Outward Bound project (HSBC/OB) is an initiative that began in September 2003 and is due to run for five years. Funded by HSBC in the Community[1] and developed and run, in part, by Outward Bound Options,[2] the program is intended to promote young people's personal and social development through physical activity. Each year, the project funds a series of residential outdoor/adventurous activity experiences for 150 pupils (aged 13–14 years) from five schools in the deprived Docklands area of London (which is adjacent to HSBC's new UK head office), and these are designed (by Outward Bound) to provide individual and group challenges and to develop skills relating to team building, communication and responsibility. After an initial residential week, there is an additional weekend event (50 pupils), and a three-week Outward Bound Classic Course[3] (10 pupils) for those individuals who are perceived to have gained the most from the earlier experiences. All pupils, however, remain involved in general follow-up activities. HSBC in the Community perceive their involvement in the project to be a 'philanthropic exercise', recognizing the value of creating links between themselves and the local community. A number of HSBC staff are involved in the project each year as volunteer mentors and are trained by informal educators,[4] based at one of the project schools, to work with the schools and pupils both within the structured activity sessions and in any additional follow-up activities within the school and local community.

### Similarities and differences between the programs

Both programs share similar aims and design features, namely: they are funded by corporate sponsors and are targeted at disaffected young people; the sponsors also fund the independent evaluations of the programs; and both are attempting to use physical activity as a means of re-engaging young people within their schools and communities. However, it is also important to note some key differences between the initiatives. First, LfS is a national program and schools can apply to participate on an annual basis, whereas the HSBC/OB project is a five-year intervention involving one group of five schools. Second, LfS has limited funding provided for a short-term program, while the HSBC/OB project is based on developing an enduring relationship with local schools. Third, LfS is linked closely to behavior improvement strategies in schools, whereas the HSBC/OB project has broader personal development aspirations for pupils. Finally, LfS is largely teacher/school-led, whereas the involvement of volunteer mentors and professional outdoor activity leaders in the HSBC/OB project means that teacher involvement (in the activity sessions at least) is minimized.

## Methods

It has been noted that it is notoriously difficult to generate 'credible' data in this type of evaluation research. In particular, researchers are wary about the reliability of the anecdotal accounts that tend to prevail (Long et al. 2002) and the challenges faced in determining causality between project and impact (Granger 1998). Recognition of these concerns has underpinned the development of the theoretical and methodological frameworks for evaluating the LfS and HSBC/OB programs. Although these two projects are different in some respects, they share sufficient common ground to warrant similar evaluation research designs. However, within the broad remit of the programs' aims, schools have flexibility in the ways in which they interpret the criteria to meet the needs of their particular pupils and schools. Thus, it has been impossible to collect pre/post data within a tightly specified framework. Instead, a range of predominantly qualitative research methods have been employed to gather data and to evaluate the impact of these projects on all participants.

Data are collected using individual pupil profiling, participant observation, semi-structured reflective journals, individual interviews, focus groups and structured feedback sheets. A dynamic and multi-layered evaluation strategy is adopted for both projects. At the heart of this strategy is the generation of pupil profiles. Long et al. (2002) have commented that, in order to ascertain whether change has occurred, it is necessary to secure baseline data on all participants at the outset of an evaluation. As such, school staff are asked to provide a brief profile for each pupil (e.g. data relating to their attendance, attitude or general behavior within school) before the start of project activities, which is then updated from the baseline at intervals. The information generated through the various research methods is collated and then analysed through a systematic grounded theory process whereby raw data (e.g. interview transcripts, fieldnotes, journals, etc.) are coded in stages (Glaser and Strauss 1967) in order to generate and verify key themes and categories (Charmaz 2000). Data are also configured around case studies and profiles of individual participants, small groups and schools.

# Findings

In this section we identify some key issues that have arisen through the evaluation process using four case studies, each one illustrating aspects of program impact on some of the schools/participants. In selecting these particular case studies, we have attempted to highlight the variety of data sources that are drawn upon within both evaluation projects.

## Case study 1: Church Lane School, Tyne and Wear (LfS – year 1)

Church Lane School, a non-selective community school in North-East England, became involved in the first year of the Living for Sport project and subsequently extended their participation into year 2. The lead teacher, Susan, involved pupils in selecting swimming, trampolining, golf, rock-climbing and archery as their project activities. The young people, who had all been selected because they were underachieving and lacking in confidence, chose to organize and run a rounders (a game similar to softball/baseball) tournament for year 4 pupils (aged 8–9 years) from a local primary school as their sports event. This was perceived to have been very successful, with Susan noting that 'staff at the primary school praised [our pupils] for their impeccable behavior and teaching skills ... they were fantastic ambassadors for the school'. At the end of the program, there were clear improvements noted in some of the project pupils, with Susan stating that 'the students are now evidently more confident in and around school [and] this has been observed by both staff and parents'. Pupils also felt that they had benefited from project involvement; for example, Billy said, 'I have met new people. I think we have learnt a lot from the team work and it was fun', and Anna said, 'I'm enjoying sport more now, what people think of me doesn't bother me anymore.' Although there was a general belief that the LfS project had been successful, the data provided by the lead teacher illustrated that there had been some variation in terms of individual pupil progress (Table 8.1).

## Case study 2: Rockford School, Merseyside (LfS – year 1)

Rockford School elected to participate in the first year of LfS, with project involvement being led by Peter, a learning mentor. The project involved ten pupils (aged 14 years), who were selected because they were all participating in an alternative curriculum.[5] A number of the pupils had been diagnosed with autistic spectrum disorder but all found communicating with others problematic and most had some form of learning difficulty. As such, it was felt that they could benefit from the social and collaborative nature of the LfS project. As a qualified climbing instructor, Peter chose to use his own skills and the school's climbing wall as the focus for the project. At the end of the project, Peter remarked that he was 'amazed by all the pupils ... I am very impressed with them and pleased for them ... it was quite emotional watching them do so well.' The impact on one individual was particularly memorable. At the start of the project, Holly was

Table 8.1 Personal profiles of pupils from Church Lane School before and after their involvement in a Living for Sport Project.

| Pupil | Before | After |
| --- | --- | --- |
| James | Quiet, small group of friends. Lovely, but no drive in lessons. | Remarkable change. Still quiet but assertive and more of a presence. Now has the confidence to approach adults. |
| Matthew | Bubbly lad, likes to be cool. Needs a confidence boost. | Improvements in confidence and self-esteem. Responsibility within group. Little change in attitude in lessons, and can be led astray. |
| Nick | Nice lad wants to be cool. Good talker and can be immature. Will work well with responsibility. | Has matured and is more approachable. Has confidence to approach adults. |
| Jennifer | Has been bullied, now bullies. Lacks confidence and self-esteem. Can be stroppy. | Progress made, but she still needs further support. She is less stroppy and more open, but still likes to gossip! Interpersonal relationships are not as good as they could be. |
| Chloe | Very quiet. Can be immature. Hangs back in lessons. Needs confidence boost. | Mature in group. More friendships and has joined teams. Fantastic support from parents. Talented sports person. |
| Jessica | Quiet and sweet, lacks confidence and self-esteem. Good organisation. | Occasional silliness because of increased confidence! More assertive. |
| Katie | Very quiet. Mum wants to push her forward and has been into school. Lacks confidence and self-esteem. | Dramatic change. Enjoying school. Bubbly and lively. Parents are very happy. Loves school! |

described by her learning mentor as 'shy and sulky'. It emerged that she struggled to communicate with her peers and very rarely spoke to adults. In addition, she had 'forgotten' her PE kit every week since she started secondary school and, as a result, had never participated in PE. During the case study visit, Holly was asked if she would mind talking to the researcher about the project and she obliged happily. Holly talked for about ten minutes, explaining with confidence that she was now able to communicate with adults and take more responsibility. She was observed instructing primary pupils (during the final sports event) and cooperating with the other young people in the group. She even managed to persuade one young girl to have a go at climbing when everyone else who had attempted to encourage her had failed. Peter noted that Holly's parents had also commented on the change they had noticed in her since her involvement in LfS.

### Case study 3: staff feedback on year 1 pupils (Middleton School, London) (HSBC)

A key part of the data collection process in the HSBC/OB project is the creation of an individual pupil database for each cohort at the five project schools. School staff are asked to provide baseline data for each pupil, identifying the reason for selection and providing supporting data (where available). Where no specific data is available (e.g. if pupils are perceived to be withdrawn or lacking in confidence) the teachers' professional judgements form the baseline data. Teachers update pupil profiles from the baseline at six-monthly intervals (for the first year, and then twelve-monthly) following participation in the main project activities. Table 8.2 provides an extract from the database of cohort 1 pupils at Middleton, and illustrates the intricate and varied nature of individual pupil progress.

### Case study 4: Kyle (Beckfield Road School, London) (HSBC – year 1)

Kyle was selected to participate in the first cohort of the HSBC/Outward Bound Project when he was in year 9 (13/14 years old). At the beginning of the project, Kyle was described as being impetuous and 'in need of role modelling', and his teachers hoped that his involvement in the project would allow him to gain maturity and self-discipline. Kyle was generally very confident among his peers, and was both vocal and domineering within social situations. After his initial involvement in the first residential week, there were varying reports about Kyle's progress upon his return to school. While his form tutor noted that he was still, at times, 'very aggressive and confrontational', another classroom teacher commented that he had begun to see improvements in Kyle's behavior, saying that '[Kyle] is more responsible about listening whilst I am talking to the class, [and] although he has a bit of a bad temper, he is getting better at controlling it.' The picture from school staff at six months was similar, with teachers noting Kyle's position as a leader among his peers and commenting that 'while he doesn't always use this position in a positive way [he] is now able to reflect on things and identify that there are different ways of dealing with problems'. This perceived progress, and regular attendance at group meetings within school, resulted in Kyle being selected to participate in a further residential activity weekend. In part, Kyle's teachers felt that this opportunity would enable him to gain continued 'benefit from being with a different group of people' and help him to refine his teamwork and communication skills. Following this second activity experience, feedback from Kyle's teachers became increasingly positive. At twelve months, his form tutor noted that Kyle's attendance and punctuality were very good, and the project coordinators commented that he had 'matured a lot [over] this year and is reflecting on his behavior'. Kyle's 'strong personality' was still seen to cause occasional problems, primarily because of his attitude when communicating with adults, but it was generally noted that he had much more control in this respect. At 24 months, it was reported that Kyle was 'making huge progress' and that there had been 'real character development'. He had been chosen as a school prefect,

Table 8.2 Progress of pupils from Middleton School throughout their involvement in the HSBC/OB project.

| Name | Profile | Brief progress report | | | |
|------|---------|-----------|-----------|-----------|-----------|
| | | 6 months | 12 months | 24 months | 36 months |
| Chris* | Intelligent, articulate and enthusiastic pupil. | There has been an immense impact, Chris has really thrived on the experience. | Academic progress steady. Occasional behaviour problems. Gaining confidence to do the right thing, when others are not!! | Excellent progress academically and in terms of motivation to achieve potential. Involved in school council. | Progressing but not fulfilling his potential. |
| John* | SEN level 5, shy, determined. | He completed the experience and made new friends. | A changed man! In my opinion one of the greatest impacts. Confidence and communication are vastly improved. | The greatest success story. Previously shy, underachieving and on the receiving end of some bullying. Now confident, achieving above expectations and developing very good social skills. | Outstanding improvement in quality of work and self-belief to improve achievement. |
| Richard | Is able but lacks confidence. | Has made some progress but is still quite shy. | Has been involved in minor behavioural problems at school. | Underachieving, no follow up involvement, involved in some disruption and truancy around school. | Slow progress, has lacked the determination and enthusiasm to be really successful. |

| Name | Profile | Brief progress report | | | |
|------|---------|-----------------------|---|---|---|
| | | 6 months | 12 months | 24 months | 36 months |
| Mark** | Very intelligent, has good leadership potential. | A great success, he thrived on the challenge. | Outstanding progress. Selected for Classic Course Communication, team work and leadership are outstanding. | Having started as a high achiever has done incredibly well to continue raising achievement. Has become involved in Duke of Edinburgh's and has been involved in many other community projects. | Outstanding academic progress and outstanding social skills. He went on to complete the Duke of Edinburgh's Silver award. |
| Paul | Is enthusiastic but lacks determination. | Some progress made, he enjoyed the experience. | Many behaviour problems at school. Confidence is high, but 'progress' is poor. | A boy of extremes, at times high achievement at the other end truancy and poor behavior I would argue that the OB experience is keeping him in contact with the 'light' side. | Poor progress, major truancy, underachievement. |

Notes:
*   Selected to attend the weekend residential activity week
**  Selected to attend the three-week Outward Bound Classic Course

had started to participate in the Duke of Edinburgh's Award scheme[6] and was a member of the school council. Following on from this, the last feedback (at around 30 months) received concerning Kyle indicated that his progress was such that he had been elected head boy for the school.

## Case study summary

These case studies illustrate a number of ways in which the LfS and HSBC/OB projects have had a positive impact upon some of the young people participating in them. For example, Kyle showed some positive developments in behavior and attitude and Holly displayed a marked improvement in self-esteem/confidence. However, the nature and degree of impact varied between pupils, with some pupils (e.g. Katie and John) benefiting greatly from the programs, but others (e.g. Jennifer and Paul) faring less well. This highlights that young people's experiences of the physical activity programs are highly individualized, and that there are many and varied paths to change (see Table 8.2). Moreover, while a young person may behave well within the project, they could remain disaffected in other areas of school life. The differing accounts of Kyle's form tutor and classroom teacher provide some evidence of this. It would seem, then, that these initiatives were successful *to some extent, for some pupils, under some conditions*. The question remaining, therefore, is what are the features of these projects that are most likely to lead to a positive impact on more pupils?

## Discussion

The data returned from schools suggest that many pupils are benefiting positively from their involvement in the LfS and HSBC/OB projects. For example, teachers indicated an average of 68 and 58 percent positive improvement for their pupils (year 1 and 2 respectively) six months into their involvement in the HSBC/OB project (Armour and Sandford 2005), while over 80 percent of teachers involved in year 2 of the LfS project rated their project's effectiveness as being at the positive end of a ten-point rating scale (Duncombe and Armour 2005). Findings also provide some support for the notion that physical activity programs can facilitate positive personal and social development in young people, particularly in terms of improving confidence, developing communication, teamwork and leadership skills, and encouraging behavioral improvement. However, although fewer in number, it is also instructive to highlight those examples where pupils did not benefit from involvement in these two projects and remain disaffected or disengaged within school.

As noted, the findings from the evaluations are both context- and situation-specific, and the impact of the programs on pupils is highly individualized. As such, it is necessary for project sponsors to recognize that their funding will have no guaranteed outcomes; indeed, at first glance, the outcomes might even look a little disappointing. Furthermore, there needs to be recognition that, even where improvements are noted, they will not be maintained in some cases. Thus, sponsors must be made aware, at a very early stage in the evaluation process, that impact is likely to be uneven, but that with the input of robust evaluation data through the life of a project it is possible to maximize positive outcomes by tailoring project designs to the needs of different pupils.

When asked to account for the variation of impact on pupils, teachers suggested a number of factors that can influence the effectiveness of projects, including: appropriate pupil selection (i.e. matching pupil needs with project objectives); the location/context of project activities (activities outside of school being perceived as more motivating for pupils than school-based initiatives); the involvement of 'additional adults' (e.g. mentors) to provide extra support; and establishing a positive relationship between project leader(s) and participants. As such, projects would appear to be more likely to succeed where they meet the specific needs of participating pupils; activities are new, exciting or culturally relevant; pupils are involved in key decision-making processes; direct links are made between project activities and wider social experience; and programs are developed with long-term impact in mind. Such comments reinforce findings within the research literature relating to positive youth development programs (e.g. Ennis 1999; Steer 2000) and have a number of clear implications for the structure and development of further initiatives.

In conclusion, the evidence from this research would appear to support claims that physical activity programs that seek to enhance young people's personal and social development are worthwhile. Positive impact on young people is a realistic expectation from such programs, although the way in which projects are structured needs careful consideration in order to maximize positive outcomes. Some features of effective programs have been outlined in this chapter, but we are aware that this is not an exhaustive list. If the so-called 'social problems industry' continues to encourage the funding and generation of projects such as those outlined here, it would seem pertinent to ensure that initiatives are developed around models of good practice and built for sustainability. In this way, programs will have more chance to develop and bear fruit (Long and Sanderson 2001), ultimately improving the experiences and prospects of the young people who participate in them.

## Notes

1  'HSBC in the Community' is a sub-group of the HSBC that has responsibility for promoting positive relationships between the organization and the local community.
2  Outward Bound Options is a development within the Outward Bound Trust in the UK which has been established to create more flexible outdoor education provisions for schools, youth groups, and community organizations. All Outward Bound Options programs are development around the needs of the young people involvement, offer a varied 'menu' or program alternatives, and take place in locations that are convenient and accessible for the target group.
3  The Classic Course is a flagship program for the Outward Bound Trust, and is for young people between the ages of 14 and 24 years. It runs over 21 days, and involves a packed schedule of adventure/challenge activities. Over the duration of the course, participants are encouraged to take increasing responsibility for themselves and to develop their communication and organizational skills.

4  Informal Educators seek to make use of everyday situations to create environments where learning is drawn out from participants' own experiences and beliefs (Doyle 2001). Within this particular school, the Informal Educators are youth workers who work outside of the set curriculum and facilitate pupils' learning through alternative means.

5  The particular curriculum referred to here is the Award Scheme Development and Accreditation Network (ASDAN) program. ASDAN was developed in the UK in the 1980s and is an organization that creates courses for individuals of all abilities to learn about various aspects of everyday life and generate key skills (http://www.asdan. co.uk).

6  The Duke of Edinburgh's Award is a voluntary scheme for young people aged from 14 to 25 years. Started in the UK, it is now available in over 50 countries worldwide. The scheme has three levels (Bronze, Sliver and Gold awards) and, for each of these, participants have to complete activities in four sections: Service (in the community); Physical Recreation (a sporting activity); Skill (a hobby or interest); and Expedition (on foot, cycle, horseback or water). It is widely recognized as a strong program that promotes positive youth development.

## References

Armour, K. M., and Sandford, R. A. (2005) 'Evaluation of the HSBC/Outward Bound partnership project and the HSBC Education Trust Kielder Challenge and Tall Ships projects (24 months)', unpublished manuscript, Loughborough University, Institute of Youth Sport.

Bailey, R. (2005) 'Evaluating the relationship between physical education, sport and social inclusion', *Educational Review*, 57(1): 71–90.

Burt, J. J. (1998) 'The role of kinesiology in elevating modern society', *Quest*, 50: 80–95.

Charmaz, K. (2000) 'Grounded theory: objectivist and constructionist methods', in N. K. Denzin and Y. S. Lincoln (eds), *Handbook of Qualitative Research* (2nd edn), pp. 509–36. London: Sage.

Davies, B. (2005) 'Threatening youth revisited: youth policies under New Labour', *The Encyclopaedia of Informal Education*. Retrieved 18 July 2006 from www.infed.org/archives/bernard_davies/revisiting_threatening_youth.htm

Department for Education and Skills (2003a) *Permanent Exclusions from Schools and Exclusion Appeals, England 2001/2002 Provisional*. SFR 16/2003. London: National Statistics.

Department for Education and Skills (2003b) *Pupil Absence in Schools in England 2002/3 Revised*. SFR 34/2003. London: National Statistics.

Department of Social Security (1999) *Opportunity for All: Tackling Poverty and Social Exclusion*. London: Trading Standards Office.

Doyle, M. E. (2001) 'On being an educator', in L. D. Richardson and M. Wolfe (eds), *Principles and Practice of Informed Education: Learning Through Life*, pp. 4–16. London: RoutledgeFalmer.

Duncombe, R., and Armour, K. (2005) 'YST/BSkyB "Living for Sport" Programme: Year 2 end of year report', unpublished manuscript, Loughborough University, Institute of Youth Sport.

Ennis, C. D. (1999) 'Creating a culturally relevant curriculum for disengaged girls', *Sport, Education and Society*, 4(1): 31–49.

Glaser, B. G., and Strauss, A. (1967) *The Discovery of Grounded Theory: Strategies for Qualitative Research*. Chicago: Aldine.

Granger, R. C. (1998) 'Establishing causality in evaluations of comprehensive community initiatives', in K. Fulbright-Anderson, A. C. Kubisch, and J. P. Connell (eds), *New Approaches to Evaluating Community Initiatives: Theory, Measurement and Analysis*, Vol. 2, pp. 221–46. Washington, DC: The Aspen Institute.

Hellison, D. (1995) *Teaching Responsibility through Physical Activity*. Champaign, IL: Human Kinetics.

Hellison, D., Cutforth, N., Kallusky, J., Martinek, T., Parker, M., and Stiehl, J. (2000) *Youth Development and Physical Activity: Linking Universities and Communities*. Champaign, IL: Human Kinetics.

Larson, A., and Silverman, S. J. (2005) 'Rationales and practices used by caring physical education teachers', *Sport, Education and Society*, 10(2): 175–94.

Lawson, H. A. (1999) 'Education for social responsibility: preconditions in retrospect and in prospect', *Quest*, 51: 116–49.

Long, J., and Sanderson, I. (2001) 'The social benefits of sport: where's the proof?', in C. Gratton and I. P. Henry (eds), *Sport in the City: The Role of Sport in Economic and Social Regeneration*, pp. 187–203. London: Routledge.

Long, J., Welch, M., Braham, P., Butterfield, J., and Hylton, K. (2002) *Count Me In: The Dimensions of Social Inclusion through Culture, Media and Sport*. Leeds: Leeds Metropolitan University.

Merton, B., and Parrott, A. (1999) *Only Connect: Successful Practice in Educational Work with Disaffected Young Adults*. Leicester: NIACE.

Morris, L., Sallybanks, J., Willis, K., and Makkai, T. (2003) 'Sport, physical activity and antisocial behaviour in youth', *Trends and Issues in Crime and Criminal Justice* (on-line), 249. Australian Institute of Criminology. Retrieved 18 July 2006 from http://www.aic. gov.au/publications/ tandi/tandi249.html

Pierce, N., and Hillman, J. (1998) *Wasted Youth: Raising Achievement and Tackling Social Exclusion*. London: Institute for Public Policy Research.

Pitter, R., and Andrews, D. L. (1997) 'Serving America's underserved youth: reflections on sport and recreation in an emerging social problems industry', *Quest*, 49: 85–99.

Sandford, R. A., Armour, K. M., and Warmington, P. C. (2006) 'Re-engaging disaffected youth through physical activity programs', *British Educational Research Journal*, 32: 251–71.

Smink, J. (2000) 'Foreword', in R. Klein (ed.), *Defying Disaffection: How Schools are Winning the Hearts and Minds of Reluctant Students*. Stoke on Trent: Trentham Books.

Social Exclusion Unit (2000) *National Strategy for Neighbourhood Renewal: Report of Policy Action Team 12: Young People* (on-line). Retrieved 18 July 2006 from http://www. socialexclusionunit.gov.uk/downloaddoc. asp?id=125/

Steer, R. (2000) *A Background to Youth Disaffection: A Review of Literature and Evaluation Findings from Work with Young People*. London: Community Development Foundation.

# 9 Using quality physical education to promote positive youth development in a developing nation

## Striving for peace education

*James Mandigo, John Corlett, and Andy Anderson*

### Introduction

In the final report on the International Year of Sport and Physical Education, the United Nations (2006) suggested that countries on every continent are starting to promote physical education (PE) as a way to establish a foundation for more peaceful societies. In this chapter we argue that PE programmes can be used to promote positive youth development (PYD) in conflicted developing nations. Ultimately, by using PE to promote PYD, we suggest that it may be possible to obtain the goals of peace education. Our intention is to highlight what physical educators can aspire to achieve on behalf of children and youth, and what our contribution to schools and the children who attend them, and their communities, can be. Specifically, in the present chapter we focus on the role of quality physical education (QPE) in promoting PYD and peace education.

### Quality physical education, positive youth development and peace education

The United Nations (UN) declared 2005 as the year of Sport and Physical Education. Linked to the Millennium Development Goals, the UN challenged the world to consider how PE can be a vehicle towards addressing global issues related to violence, inequality, disease, hunger, primary education, environmental sustainability and global partnerships. Similarly, at the 2nd World Summit on Physical Education, participants from over 40 countries ratified the Magglingen Commitment for Physical Education (2005). This declaration highlighted the unique role of PE in culture, health and development, and the promotion of peace throughout the world.

The promotion of peace is a relatively new challenge for PE professionals. Typically, PE has been viewed as a mechanism to provide youth with the skills to lead healthy active lives in terms of physical activity and maintaining a healthy body weight. Despite the importance of these laudable goals, PE is still one of the most marginalized subject areas in schools around the world, due to the notion that it is non-productive and non-intellectual (Hardman and Marshall 2000). However, the global community is now starting to consider the potential role of PE in providing solutions to social injustices that often undermine the stability of nations that have recently ceased armed conflicts but have yet to fully achieve a state of peacefulness.

At the Berlin World Summit on Physical Education in 1999, the characteristics of a QPE programme were endorsed by experts and delegates from around the world. Specifically, QPE programmes: (a) are child centred; (b) create a positive environment; (c) develop the skills and knowledge required to foster independence and independent learners; and (d) incorporate human rights, gender equity and peace education (International Council for Health, Physical Education, Recreation, Sport and Dance 2001a). Subsequently, international standards for QPE have addressed grade-specific benchmarks related to personal and social behaviour and understanding and respect for individual difference (International Council for Health, Physical Education, Recreation, Sport, and Dance 2001b). These international standards for QPE help to provide a foundation for children and youth to develop the knowledge, skills and attitudes for healthy development. As a result, many nations are starting to consider how to use QPE to help children and youth imbue skills associated with a becoming a truly peaceful nation (United Nations 2003).

We suggest that QPE programmes provide an ideal vehicle to foster PYD, which in turn may lead to the ultimate goal of peace education. Thus, PYD is one mechanism by which we may promote peace. In the present chapter we explore connections between QPE and Lerner *et al.*'s (2005) '5 Cs' of PYD (i.e. Competence, Confidence, Connection, Character, and Caring/ Compassion). These 5 Cs are consistent with the core foundations of healthy and positive development. A QPE programme will aim at understanding, educating and engaging children and youth in proactive and constructive ways (Damon 2004). A QPE programme adopts a holistic approach to fostering development across the four main areas of PYD as defined by the National Research Council and Institute of Medicine (2004): physical, intellectual, psychological/ emotional, and social development. Table 9.1 provides examples of the type of behaviours that can be encouraged through a QPE programme to foster PYD across each of these areas of development. By focusing upon the whole child and the complex interactions amongst the different domains of human development, QPE programmes have the potential to foster life skills related to creativity, initiative, problem-solving, critical thinking, social justice, equality and equity and leadership (United Nations 2003). These characteristics have been identified as the foundation for not only PYD (Larson 2000) but also for making, keeping, and building peaceful nations (Johnson and Johnson 2005a).

Just as health is not simply the absence of disease, peace is not *simply* about the absence of violence. Peace may be defined as 'the absence of war or violence in a mutually beneficial, harmonious relationship among relevant parties' (Johnson and Johnson 2005b: 277). In other words, not only must there be a cessation of

Table 9.1 Examples of behaviors within QPE programs that foster the development of Lerner's 5Cs across dimensions of overall human development

| | Physical | Intellectual | Psychological | Social |
|---|---|---|---|---|
| Competence | Develop a wide variety of skills that enable me to engage in healthy living activities. | Think creatively and imaginatively about how to play each game. | Value skill development as a determinant of optimal play. | Learn to play with others so each improves. |
| Confidence | Participate with confidence knowing the tactical and strategic dimensions of each game. | Apply the tactics and skills to the dynamics and artfulness of play. | Apply effort to skill and play performance. | Respect the power of collective effort. |
| Character | Play fair. | Know how optimistic efforts add to play outcomes. | Value play with others as team mates and opponents. | Recognize the value of team work. |
| Connection | Experience affiliation with others through physical pursuits. | Work with other participants to develop strategies for success. | Value camaraderie of fellow players. | Values sense of connectedness and belonging associated with group/team play. |
| Caring and Compassion | Participate to help others experience the reward of play with enthusiasm. | Play in ways that build other players' skills and confidence. | Play competitively but with humility, respect opponents and lose with dignity. | Support team/group members despite outcomes. |

open and armed conflict, but there must also exist a positive relationship between conflicting parties that recognize mutual benefits and social justice grounded in a shared environment characterized by calm, tranquillity, order and harmony. Johnson and Johnson suggested that the ultimate goal of peace education is 'for individuals to be able to maintain peace among aspects of themselves (intrapersonal peace), individuals (interpersonal peace), groups (intergroup peace), and countries, societies, and cultures (international peace)' (2005b: 276).

Ennis *et al.* (1999) created a high school PE curriculum reform titled 'Sport for Peace' which was intended to enhance students' interactions and engagement. Results from their ethnographic evaluation study showed that the Sport for Peace model fostered shared responsibility for learning, trust, respect, a sense of family, and an atmosphere for engagement and participation. Thus, there is some evidence that integrating principles of peace education into PE curricula may have a positive impact on intrapersonal, interpersonal and intergroup peace. By attempting to foster PYD through QPE we believe that goals relating to intrapersonal, interpersonal and intergroup peace may be obtained.

## Using QPE to promote PYD and peace education in El Salvador

El Salvador is a nation with unique challenges: struggling with democracy after a brutal civil war that left a legacy of gang violence still much in evidence, with a national homicide rate that is ten times the global average; 20 percent of its citizens living abroad, creating economic and social instability; and a growing population of children and youth whose futures depend on the choices they learn to make under difficult circumstances (Pan American Health Organization 1998). For many children and their families, thoughts about the future are shrouded in the despair of violence in their communities. In a recent report, 20 percent of adolescents in El Salvador had been threatened or injured with a weapon while 32 percent of adolescents reported feelings of sadness/hopelessness (Springer *et al.* 2006). Schools play an important role in the peace process as they provide a safe haven in which children can experience peace and be provided with the opportunity to develop the life skills that enable them to make peace an integral part of their lives at school and in their communities.

To help combat these issues around social justice, the Ministry of Education in El Salvador launched a 15-year national public plan in March 2005 (called Plan 2021) aimed towards the modernization of its education system. PE in school communities has since been identified as a pathway for children and youth to develop the competence and confidence associated with skills related to peace-making and leading ultimately to peace-building. Programmes for healthy development emphasize participation in a wide variety of play experiences that enable young people to form identities of courage, compassion, and cooperation. Working constructively and cooperatively with learning partners (parents, teachers, community care providers, peers), they can also experience feelings of connection – a deeper sense of belonging, care and hope. Ultimately, young people build connections within self and others by 'expecting more'. Through creative challenges, students can expect to have a hand in change, expect their talents to help them learn, expect that working together builds character, respect and capacity of innovation, and expect their hard work to contribute to the growth of their nation. These goals are closely aligned with Lerner *et al.*'s (2005) 5 Cs model.

## A QPE programme for El Salvador

In developing a QPE programme within El Salvador, the authors have been working with local stakeholders since 2005 to develop a comprehensive approach under the programme banner Scotiabank Salud Escolar Integral (Scotiabank Building Healthy Students). If schools are to provide the educational foundation for healthy development, they must model the integration of the many faces of health as fully as possible into the school experience (Corlett 1986; Flay 2002; World Health Organization 1998). The links between good health and favourable education outcomes are clear. Children who enjoy good health are more likely to engage whole-heartedly in academic and non-academic programmes and school community activities (Allensworth *et al.* 1997) and are more likely to develop into healthy adults upon whom healthy communities can be built (World Health Organization 1999).

Although many existing PE curricula around the world include elements of cooperation or social responsibility, the focus in most countries is still upon skill mastery and fitness to support a competitive sports-dominated and performance-related activity programme (Hardman and Marshall 2005; Jewett 1989). Accordingly, we drew from Hellison's (1984) humanistic approach when implementing the QPE curriculum to provide a consistent link with PYD and peace education. A humanistic approach to PE involves 'a concern for man above all else behaviourally and concern for man's social and emotional well-being' (Hellison 1973: 3). The goals of a QPE curriculum that adopts a humanistic approach include the development of self-esteem, self-actualization, self-understanding, and positive interpersonal relations with others. These values help students to make their own self–body–world connection, provide a sense of community and facilitate a playful spirit (Jewett and Bain 1985).

The Scotiabank Salud Escolar Integral in El Salvador is helping to create a QPE programme by redesigning the national PE curriculum to create educational experiences that promote healthy development and healthy choices. It provides hope, skills and opportunities for a successful future which in turn are critical throughout the peace-building process. The programme has five main action areas that focus upon working with strategic local stakeholders to ensure the necessary infrastructure is built within El Salvador to achieve the vision of the programme. These action areas are: (a) professional development; (b) practical demonstrations in schools and community settings; (c) professional collaboration; (d) curriculum development at national and university level; and, (e) youth leadership.

The signature piece of the Scotiabank Salud Escolar Integral programme is the first action area of Professional Development which consists of a week-long series of workshops conducted by several Canadian experts representing various education sectors (universities, colleges and public schools). Throughout the week, pre-service teachers from the local university and in-service teachers from across El Salvador take part in a number of 'theory into practice' training sessions. To date, a total of 13 workshops, with close to 1000 pre-service and in-service teachers, have been conducted. The workshops have provided a mix of theoretical and practical examples of how QPE can be a vehicle to helping children and youth develop skills to make healthy choices that are consistent with the development of the 5 Cs of PYD and the Millennium Development Goals.

Consider the following activity that was used during one of the workshops with in-service teachers called 'Crossing the Volcano'. This is a common cooperative game that requires groups of five or six to reach the other end of the gymnasium by only using a limited number of pieces of equipment (e.g. a hula hoop, skipping rope, frisbee, cone, etc.). All members of the group must work together to make it safely to the other side without stepping onto the floor ('the volcano lava') by only stepping on the four or five pieces of equipment that are initially provided. Once all members of a team safely reach the opposite end of the gymnasium with their equipment, one piece of equipment is removed and they must return to the other side of the gymnasium. Subsequent trips are also made more difficult by removing pieces of equipment. As more pieces of equipment are taken away, participants often report more enjoyment of the activity and increased reliance upon their teammates. So how does this fun and challenging activity help to promote the development of the Millennium Development Goals through PYD?

For a developing country to continue to develop and to move towards peace-building there must be a shared vision and goal to work towards a better and brighter future. In Crossing the Volcano, if one person decides to work individually, the other members of the team are left stranded in the volcano and the end result is failure. However, by working together (Connection) and by ensuring that *everyone* reaches the other side successfully (Caring/Compassion), teams increase their chances of success (Competence). This in turn develops a sense of Confidence to tackle more difficult tasks when resources become scarce and individuals soon discover the abilities and potentials of themselves and others that they had never realized possible (Character). Through this simple cooperative game, a conversation is started about how working together can lead to sustainable development and equality for all.

The other four action areas of the Scotiabank Salud Escolar Integral programme are intended to provide an infrastructure in which teachers are supported in delivering a QPE curriculum that is consistent with peace education and where children and youth will have the opportunity to apply the skills they have learned both within and outside of the school environment. Under the action area of Practical Demonstrations, members of the Canadian delegation have visited a number of schools to provide practical demonstrations and lessons with students. Equipment and other resources are often left behind to provide some minimal resources for teachers at the school to continue with the implementation of what many perceive as initially novel yet effective ways to deliver QPE. The reaction to such an approach is often very positive and inspiring. On a recent visit to El Salvador, members of the Canadian delegation conducted a demonstration with teachers and students at a local school only five blocks from the centre of the gang violence in San Salvador. The activities incorporated the 5 Cs into a number of physical activities that were geared around fostering literacy and numeracy. At the end of the demonstration with one class and the rest of the school watching, it soon became apparent that the entire school community wanted to participate. With a quick modification, close to 300 teachers and students were soon all participating together in a dance activity that everyone (kindergarten to grade 8) could do successfully and with confidence. At the conclusion of the demonstration, one of the young students at the school was overheard telling her principal that she wished they could participate in a PE class like this every day.

Within the action area of Curriculum Development, a revision of the existing national PE curriculum in El Salvador, is in its beginning phase. Initial discussions with government officials have addressed the need to develop a national QPE program that will focus upon the development of life skills associated with PYD through peace education. To prepare future teachers to implement this unique programme, a new undergraduate programme in PE has recently been approved by the Ministry of Education and was implemented in January, 2007 at Pedagógica University with an initial cohort of 50 students. The pedagogy to be used to prepare teachers to implement the revised QPE curriculum in schools and to prepare student-teachers studying at university-based programs in El Salvador will be consistent with the basic tenets of peace education.

Support for in-service teachers is also being planned within the fourth action area of Professional Collaboration. A new regional PE association in Santa Ana (a district within El Salvador) has been formed with a vision towards becoming a national PE association synonymous with other national associations such as the Canadian Association for Health, Physical Education, Recreation and Dance. Recognizing an opportunity to provide support for all physical educators in El Salvador, the Scotiabank Salud Escolar Integral programme has dedicated resources to support the creation and early development of this important group of local experts and plans are currently underway for a National Physical Education conference to be organized and delivered by region experts within the year.

The fifth action area of the Scotiabank Salud Escolar Integral programme is that of Youth Leadership. Given the challenges of working directly with youth in El Salvador due to security concerns, language barriers and sensitivities to cultural needs, the strategy to date has been to provide support and resources for those working directly with children and youth throughout the country. This has included not only teachers within schools, but also youth leaders working with other governmental ministries (e.g. Youth Secretariat, National Security Council) and local NGOs (e.g. Plan El Salvador). These youth leaders work in both urban and underserviced rural areas where they are often respected by local gangs. Plan El Salvador works with disadvantaged children and their families to teach basic skills such as cooking, growing vegetables and reading. They often use games as a way to bring children and youth together. The Scotiabank Salud Escolar Integral programme helps to provide training for the Plan Leaders to support the use of physical activities as vehicles for developing skills consistent with the 5 Cs of PYD. Plans are also under way to host a national Unity Games: the vision is for children and youth from across El Salvador to come together for a day to participate in activities that have been designed and delivered by youth leaders under the umbrella of Unity. Activities that foster critical elements of respect, tolerance, and equality will be central themes.

## Evaluation and monitoring

The evaluation and monitoring of the QPE programme in El Salvador has been limited to date. Table 9.2 provides an overview of the number of participants that have been exposed to the programme. The only other source of formative evaluation has been anecdotal information arising from small-group conversations. For example, on a recent visit to El Salvador, the authors asked a school principal: 'What does Physical Education mean to your school?' Her reply was simply: 'My students never miss a day when they have PE class.' We later asked a group of PE teachers the same question. Some of the replies were: 'Physical education is the soul of the school', 'Through physical education, we foster good health and a good society', 'Physical education is the means to develop social happiness', 'Physical education contributes to development as a human being', 'Physical education provides opportunities to integrate all students' and 'Physical education is the soul to give life to the youth.' Such powerful statements by education leaders within El Salvador highlight the potential that QPE can have upon a developing country.

Senior government officials within the Ministry of Education, Youth Secretariat, Security Council and the vice-president's office have also commented on the importance of this QPE programme for the future of El Salvador. In a follow-up meeting with one such official which took place eight months after the inaugural workshops in 2005, he told a story of a young boy who attended a school where his PE teacher had just returned from one of the workshops. The young boy was labelled as being at risk, due to the violent and aggressive behaviours that he had been exhibiting. Upon the teacher's return, he began to incorporate within his PE class the core elements from the workshops that incorporated many of Lerner's 5 Cs for PYD. The senior government official went on to say that, after a few classes, the young boy soon realized the dangers of his actions for himself and for others (i.e. a recognition of unhealthy choices) and came to apologize to his teacher for his previous behaviour. Although we were not in a position to validate this story, it does provide some insight into the potential impact of the QPE programme.

The QPE programme has also had a positive impact upon the team of Canadian teachers who have travelled to El Salvador. One of the team members (a Canadian administrator) said:

> It was an amazing learning experience for me on so many levels and I was truly inspired by all of you and by the unique and valuable role that each of you brings to the team. I was almost moved to tears by how deeply the impact

*Table 9.2* Scotiabank Salud Escolar Integral – measurement metrics (by year).

| Activities | 2005 | 2006 | 2007 (Projected) |
|---|---|---|---|
| Canadian universities involved | 2 | 3 | 4 |
| Salvadoran universities involved | 2 | 1 | 1 |
| Salvadoran government ministries involved | 1 | 2 | 3 |
| NGOs in El Salvador involved | 0 | 1 | 2 |
| Meetings with Salvadoran Ambassador in Ottawa | 0 | 2 | 3 |
| Meetings with Canadian Ambassador in El Salvador | 1 | 3 | 5 |
| Meetings with Cabinet Ministers in El Salvador | 1 | 1 | 3 |
| Workshops delivered in El Salvador | 1 | 11 | 15 |
| Teachers at workshops | 1000 | 192 | 800 |
| School visits | 4 | 2 | 8 |
| Presentations at schools | 1 | 1 | 5 |
| Salvadoran children who have participated | 30 | 340 | 500 |
| Canadian experts in El Salvador | 7 | 7 | 10 |
| External grants applied For | 1 | 2 | 2 |
| Successful external grants | 0 | 1 | - |
| Press conferences | 1 | 2 | 3 |
| Press releases | 1 | 2 | 4 |
| Number of interviews | 1 | 5 | 10 |
| Cost of equipment distributed | $500 | $800 | $1500 |
| Special events (e.g., National Unity Games) | 0 | 0 | 1 |
| Children attending special national events | 0 | 0 | 500 |
| International Presentations | 0 | 2 | 2 |
| National presentations (Canada) | 0 | 1 | 2 |
| National presentations (El Salvador) | 0 | 1 | 2 |
| Provincial presentations (Ontario) | 0 | 6 | 10 |
| Local presentations (Niagara) | 0 | 1 | 2 |
| Visits to Canada by Salvadoran educators | 0 | 3 | 5 |
| Curriculum and policy development initiatives | 0 | 1 | 2 |

of physical activity could be notably seen and actually felt in each workshop, class and school setting where you all realized the powerful tool of PE.

As this quote suggests, the benefits of such a programme span international boundaries and make all of us involved in the project more connected, confident, compassionate, and caring when it comes to the impact of PE. Despite this project's relative novelty and short time frame to date, the energy and passion that has both driven and will continue to drive this programme from both countries has been truly inspirational. However, we clearly need future research grounded in sound methodologies and theoretical frameworks to evaluate the impact of the QPE programme. PYD has provided a solid conceptual framework to developing and implementing El Salvador's QPE programme that is entrenched within peace education. These theories will also provide frameworks for the future evaluation of the programme on the healthy development of children, youth, teachers, stakeholders, and other members of the school community.

## QPE, PYD, and peace education: a bridge too far?

The ideological meanings of education for peace pertain to a social, cultural, and political way of life that nurtures conditions that enable individuals and communities to live in harmony rather than discord. We have proposed an orientation to curriculum and instruction for QPE that methodologically and pedagogically brings to life core principals of human development set out by these perspectives on peace (e.g. an innate desire to learn about and to help others, to be treated with dignity and respect and to treat others the same way). The Millennium Development Goals and United Nations Declaration of Human Rights are clear: all children have the right to education, good health, and the right to live free from oppression and violence.

For physical educators working in peaceful, developed nations with well-established PE curricula and an understanding that PE belongs in our schools, it is a humbling revelation to become engaged in the work of our profession in a nation like El Salvador. Our reflections on and subsequent work with other developing countries in education for peace through QPE emphasize that educational experiences should activate students' abilities and opportunities to interact with each other. Such interactions take the form of promoting students' abilities to construct knowledge, solve problems to use their talents creatively and, through acts of kindness, empathy, compassion and cooperation, contribute directly to changes in their environment. Consistent with the work by Hellison *et al.* (2000) on the importance of linking universities and communities together, we regard our collaborative work with our partners as existing within a grander scheme that acknowledges our professional responsibilities much more broadly than service provision and employment. We hold the belief that as physical educators, this approach *is worth doing* and we are part of a world-wide family who have a shared responsibility to foster positive human development.

## References

Allensworth, D. E., Lawson, L. Nicholson and Wyche, J. (1997) *Schools and Health: Our Nation's Investment*. Washington, DC: National Academy Press.

Corlett, J. T. (1986) 'The role of physical education in the intellectual and social enhancement of children in developing countries', *Physical Education Review*, 9(1): 28–30.

Damon, W. (2004) 'What is positive youth development?', *Annals of the American Academy of Political and Social Science*, 591: 13–24

Ennis, C. D., Solmon, M. A., Satina, S., Loftus, S. J., Mensch, J., McCauley, M. T. (1999) 'Creating a sense of family in urban schools using the "Sport for Peace" curriculum', *Research Quarterly for Exercise and Sport*, 70: 273–85.

Flay, B. R. (2002) 'Positive youth development requires comprehensive health programs', *American Journal of Health Behavior*, 26: 407–24.

Hardman, K., and Marshall, J. (2000) 'The state and status of physical education in schools in international context', *European Physical Education Review*, 3: 203–29.

Hardman, K., and Marshall, J. (2005) 'Update on the status of physical education worldwide', keynote address at 2nd World Summit on Physical Education, Magglingen, Switzerland.

Hellison, D. (1973) *Humanistic Physical Education*. Englewood Cliffs, NJ: Prentice-Hall.

Hellison, D. (1984) *Goals and Strategies for Teaching Physical Education*. Champaign, IL: Human Kinetics.

Hellison, D., Cutforth, N., Kallusky, J., Martinek, T., Parker, M., and Stiehl, J. (2000) *Youth Development and Physical Activity*. Champaign, IL: Human Kinetics.

International Council for Health, Physical Education, Recreation, Sport and Dance (2001a) *World Summit on Physical Education*. Berlin, Germany: Author.

International Council for Health, Physical Education, Recreation, Sport and Dance (2001b) *International Standards for Physical Education and Sport for School Children* (online). Retrieved 25 July 2006 from http://www. ichpersd.org/i/children.html

International Council of Sport Science and Physical Education (2005) Magglingen Commitment for Physical Education. Presented at the 2nd World Summit on physical education: Magglingen, Switzerland (December 2–3). Retrieved 22 September 2006 from http://www.who.int/moveforhealth/publications/PAH_2nd_world_summit_2005_en.pdf.

Jewett, A. E. (1989) 'Curriculum theory in physical education', *International Review of Education*, 35: 35–49.

Jewett, A. E., and Bain, L. L. (1985) *The Curriculum Process in Physical Education*. Dubuque, IA: William Brown.

Johnson, D. W., and Johnson, R. T. (2005a) 'Essential components of peace education', *Theory into Practice*, 44: 280–92.

Johnson, D. W., and Johnson, R. T. (2005b) 'This issue: peace education', *Theory into Practice*, 44: 275–9.

Larson, R. W. (2000) 'Toward a psychology of positive youth development', *American Psychologist*, 55: 170–83.

Lerner, R. M., Lerner, J. V., Almerigi, J. B., Theokas, C., Phelps, E., Nadeau, S., *et al.* (2005) 'Positive youth development, participation in community youth development programs, and community contributions of fifth-grade adolescents: findings from the first wave of the 4-H study of positive youth development', *Journal of Early Adolescence*, 25: 17–71.

Magglingen Commitment for Physical Education (2005) 2nd World Summit on Physical Education: Magglingen, Switzerland (2–3 Dec.). Retrieved 22 Sept. 2006 from http://www.who.int/moveforhealth/publications/ PAH_2nd_world_summit_2005_en.pdf

National Research Council and Institute of Medicine (2004) *Brief Report: Community Programs to Promote Youth Development*. Retrieved 1 Aug. 2006 from http://www7.nationalacademies.org/bocyf/youth_development _brief.pdf

Pan American Health Organization (1998) *Health in the Americas*, vol. 2. Washington, DC: Author.

Springer, A. E., Selwyn, B. J., and Kelder, S. H. (2006) 'A descriptive study of youth risk behavior in urban and rural secondary school students in El Salvador', *BMC International Health and Human Rights*, 6(3). Retrieved 20 Nov. 2006 from http://www.pubmedcentral.nih.gov/picrender. fcgi? artid=1459212andblobtype=pdf

United Nations (2003) *Sport for Development and Peace: Towards Achieving the Millennium Development Goals*. Report from the United Nations Inter-Agency Task Force for Sport for Development and Peace. New York: United Nations.

United Nations (2006) *Report on the International Year of Sport and Physical Education*. Geneva: United Nations. Retrieved 20 Nov. 2006 from http://www.sportanddev.org/data/document/document/256.pdf

World Health Organization (1998) *Health-Promoting Schools: A Healthy Setting for Living, Learning and Working.* Geneva: WHO.

World Health Organization (1999) *Improving Health through Schools: National and International Strategies.* Geneva: WHO.

# 10 Future directions for positive youth development and sport research

## Nicholas L. Holt and Martin I. Jones

## Introduction

This chapter is intended to draw together some of the issues raised in this book. First, salient features associated with instructional sport programs are discussed with a view to identifying areas for future research. Second, in the interests of providing some balance, selected marginal and/or negative outcomes associated with sport participation are considered. Throughout, suggestions for future research which may help advance the area of PYD through sport are presented.

## Instructional sport PYD programs

As many of the contributors to this book have shown, there is widespread belief that sport can be used as a vehicle to promote physical activity and PYD. Several authors presented instructional programs to promote PYD using sport (Chapters 4, 5, and 6), physical activity (Chapter 8), and physical education (Chapter 9). In contrast to many regular organized sports, these instructional programs have been specifically designed to promote PYD. The goals of these programs are congruent with PYD, and the programs are generally delivered in a manner consistent with the guidelines provided by the US National Research Council Institute of Medicine (2002). The contributors have also revealed some emerging evidence for the efficacy of these instructional sport-based PYD programs. Nonetheless, given that the field is still in its infancy, much work remains to be done. In particular, the field requires more studies to evaluate the efficacy and effectiveness of specific interventions. Carefully designed studies will enable researchers to establish what types of sport-based interventions work, with which populations, and under what conditions.

One approach that may provide a useful direction for advancing PYD research is Greenwald and Cullen's (1985) translational framework. They suggested that there are five phases of translational research: (1) basic research, (2) methods development, (3) efficacy trials, (4) effectiveness trials, and (5) dissemination trials. In phase 1, basic research involves the generation of explanatory models and findings that can inform the design of intervention components. During phase 2, research and intervention methods needed to apply basic concepts to an applied setting are developed. This can include the feasibility testing of novel interventions based on basic behavioral science findings. Phase 3 involves efficacy trials with a fairly high degree of control to maximize internal validity. Phase 4 involves effectiveness trials: the implementation and testing of intervention programs in real-world conditions. Phase 5 translation involves the evaluation of conditions that facilitate or impede the widespread distribution and adoption of the intervention.

There is an emerging body of basic research which has revealed connections between sport and positive (and negative) outcomes. Consequently, much of the work conducted by the authors of Chapters 4, 5, 6, 8, and 9 could be described as the development of novel research and intervention methods to apply basic concepts in applied settings. Given the inherently applied nature of sport, it is difficult to conduct strictly controlled trials. However, some phase 3 efficacy-type trials have been conducted. For example, Papacharisis *et al.* (2004) evaluated an adapted version of the SUPER program with Greek children. Results revealed that, compared to a control group, participants in the experimental group demonstrated greater knowledge of life skills, higher self-beliefs for goal setting, problem-solving, and positive thinking, and performed better on sport-specific tasks. In addition to continued attempts to demonstrate the efficacy of novel interventions, in the future we also anticipate that we will see more effectiveness trials whereby instructional programs are tested in real-world conditions. For example, the SUPER program could be delivered to young athletes competing in existing sport leagues. Participants could be randomized into control and intervention groups in order to assess the effectiveness of the intervention. If the 'real-world' effectiveness of interventions can be demonstrated, we would expect to see more phase 5 dissemination work.

We are essentially calling for more evaluation of sport PYD programs. In this respect, it may be useful to consider some of the lessons learned in evaluating 'non-sport' youth development programs, which is a field of scholarship with a longer history than the sport-based research into PYD. In their review of youth development programs in the US, Roth and Brooks-Gunn (2003) identified several methodological issues that had constrained program evaluation. Primarily, the methods and outcomes used to evaluate youth programs had often been inadequate for understanding if and why a program positively impacted youth. Few programs involved comprehensive evaluations, including experimental (or even quasi-experimental) designs that combined questions of implementation and outcomes. To advance sport-based PYD research it will be important to combine implementation questions (i.e. questions about specific programming elements, duration of involvement, and staffing issues) with questions about the positive *and* negative outcomes associated with program involvement. Moreover, adequate descriptions of the population served, the intervention, and implementation procedures are needed to allow replication of sport-based PYD research and to allow researchers and practitioners to make inferences about the benefits of intervention strategies and implementation procedures (Catalano *et al.* 1999).

Another concern for youth development program evaluation has been the lack of reliable and valid measures of positive behaviors (Roth and Brooks-Gunn 2003). However, in recent years some measures have been developed, such as the Youth Experience Survey (YES, 2.0) (Larson et al. 2006), and Lerner et al.'s (2005) battery of questionnaires to assess the '5Cs' of PYD, which could be used by researchers to examine PYD in a sporting context. Sport researchers may also be able to adapt evaluation approaches from the developmental psychology literature. For example, Akiva (2005) presented the High/Scope Youth Program Quality Assessment (PQA) tool, which was based on a four-year validation study. The PQA involves an ongoing assessment of program quality and improvement based on the presence of participatory polices and procedures, a safe environment, a supportive environment, youth–adult interaction, and youth engagement. The adoption of the PQA and other evaluative approaches may help to advance sport-based PYD research.

Long-term evaluation is crucial for understanding how participation in sport-based PYD programs influences transitions from adolescence into adulthood. Important questions to consider are as follows. Do skills learned through instructional sport-based programs transfer to other life areas? How do instructional sport-based programs influence family functioning? What are the processes through which adolescents attain positive developmental outcomes? Do adolescents who engage in instructional sport-based PYD programs experience healthier development than adolescents enrolled in other types of program? Are developmental outcomes learned through sport maintained over time? Do outcomes remain after the sport program is removed? These questions (and many others) may represent important future research directions for instructional sport-based PYD programs.

## Organized 'everyday' youth sport programs

As highlighted in the introductory chapter and reflected by the structure of this book, it is important to distinguish between instructional programs that have stated goals consistent with the values of PYD and regular 'everyday' youth sport programs, which may or may not have any stated developmental goals. These regular everyday youth sport programs represent the type of sporting involvement in which the majority of young people engage. It is also important that researchers, practitioners, coaches, and youth leaders acknowledge that both positive and negative outcomes have been associated with participation in youth sport. Based on a recent review of the literature, Morris et al. (2003) concluded that there is a lack of robust evidence for the direct, sustained impact of sport participation on positive development. In this section we wish to comment on selected positive and negative outcomes associated with sport participation in the interests of providing a 'balanced' perspective on the role of youth sport in promoting PYD.

Larson et al. (2006) used the YES (2.0) to examine the types of developmental and negative experiences 2280 US 11th graders associated with their participation in sports, performance and fine arts, academic clubs, community-oriented activities, service activities, and faith-based youth activities. Sports stood out from other activities as a context for experiences relating to the development of initiative (i.e. sustaining effort and setting goals, and learning to push oneself), emotional regulation, and teamwork experiences. These findings for positive experiences in sport are broadly consistent with results from previous studies (e.g. Dworkin *et al.* 2003; Hansen *et al.* 2003). Sport participation has also been associated with other positive development outcomes, including academic achievement (Marsh and Kleitman 2003), reduced use of illegal drugs (Kulig *et al.* 2003), engaging in fewer risky sexual behaviors (Miller *et al.* 2002), and protection from depression (Boone and Leadbeater 2006).

In assessing the processes underpinning these positive experiences, it may be that organized sport is 'naturally suited' to producing certain positive outcomes (Holt 2007; Holt *et al.* 2006). For example, coaches typically emphasize the importance of hard work and pushing oneself through sport (Holt and Dunn 2004). This may explain why the development of initiative has been associated with sport participation. Athletes may learn to regulate emotion through sport because it is a context in which they must learn to deal with stress in order to be effective performers (Nicholls *et al.* 2005). It may also follow that those athletes who do not learn to regulate their emotions actually withdraw from sport to pursue other endeavors (Petlichkoff 1996). Finally, learning to work together as a team, and dealing with challenges relating to teamwork, is a central component of many sporting experiences (Holt and Sparkes 2001).

There are clearly numerous advantages associated with sport participation, and at the present time the evidence indicates that the positives outweigh the negatives. However, we maintain that it is important to recognize that sport has also been associated with some negative and/or marginal outcomes. For example, a study conducted in the UK showed that males with high levels of sport involvement were 1.7 times more likely to engage in delinquent behaviors at the age of 18 than males with low levels of sport involvement (Begg *et al.* 1996). In the same study, when compared to a low sport involvement group of females, moderately and highly involved females were 2.3 and 2.7 times respectively more likely to be involved in delinquent behaviors at the age of 18. To provide a balanced perspective on the potential role of sport in promoting PYD, two further negative/marginal issues that have been associated with sport participation will be addressed; namely the use of alcohol and tobacco.

## Sport participation and alcohol use

Participation in sports is positively correlated with high use of alcohol among athletes of both genders from several countries, including France (Lorente *et al.* 2004; Peretti-Watel *et al.* 2003), the US (Rainey *et al.* 1996), and Iceland (Thorlindsson 1989). Interestingly, use of alcohol appears to be most prevalent among adolescents who participate in team sports (e.g. Perreti-Watel *et al.* 2002). Based on results of a longitudinal study of US adolescents, Eccles and Barber (1999) found that participation in team sports was associated with positive educational trajectories but high frequencies of drinking alcohol. In a follow-up study, Eccles *et al.* (2003) found that at grade 12 male and female athletes reported being drunk more than non-athletes, and being involved in team sports predicted significant increases in alcohol use and getting drunk over the high school years after controlling for gender, intellectual aptitude, and mother's education. Therefore, adolescent athletes, particularly athletes involved in team sports, appear to use alcohol more than non-athletes.

## Sport participation and tobacco use

Overall, athletes appear to be less likely to *regularly* smoke cigarettes than non-athletes (Baumert *et al.* 1998; Pate *et al.* 2000; Peretti-Watel *et al.* 2002; Rainey *et al.* 1996; Rodriguez and Audrain-McGovern 2004; Thorlindsson 1989). Experimentation with smoking usually begins during adolescence, and team sport participation during this period can protect against the progression from experimentation to regular smoking (Audrain-McGovern *et al.* 2006; Donato *et al.* 1997). Further evidence for the protective effects of sport is based on the observation that adolescents with decreasing or erratic team sport participation patterns are almost three times more likely to become regular smokers than adolescents with consistently high team sport participation (Rodriquez and Audrain-McGovern 2004). However, when different uses of tobacco have been dissected, findings show that adolescent athletes in the US were more likely to report use of smokeless tobacco products (e.g. chewing tobacco) even after controlling for other variables (Davis *et al.* 1997; Garry and Morrissey 2000; Melnick *et al.* 2001; Pate *et al.* 2000). Thus, whereas sport may protect against regular cigarette smoking, US adolescent athletes appear to engage in the use of smokeless tobacco more than non-athletes.

## Sport as a risk factor?

Based on the evidence cited above, a plausible conclusion is that sport participation may be a risk factor for the use of alcohol and smokeless tobacco. To better understand how to promote positive outcomes through sport, it may be worthwhile to consider why some negative outcomes have been associated with sport participation. Although the processes underlying these patterns of alcohol and tobacco use have not been formally assessed, several speculative explanations have been provided. For example, Audrain-McGovern *et al.* (2006) provided two explanations for the protective effects of sport against regular cigarette smoking. The first explanation, based on a psycho-physiological perspective, is that the physical activity associated with team sport participation may provide a 'reward' by increasing dopamine (a chemical neurotransmitter involved in the formation of emotional responses and the perception of pain and pleasure) levels, thus reducing the need to smoke as a reward (cf. Esch and Stefano 2004). Alternatively, on a more social-psychological level, they suggested that the social reinforcement of not smoking within the athletic subculture may offset any adolescent propensity to smoke.

Social norms of sport participation may be at the heart of the matter. In particular, peer group identity formation may influence adolescents' choices, whereby being a member of a certain group (e.g. a sport team) helps structure the choices adolescents make (Eccles *et al.* 2003). For example, in certain sports and certain regions (e.g. football in southern USA), sport participation may be synonymous with the use of smokeless tobacco (i.e. 'everyone chews'). In a similar way, the use and misuse of alcohol among adolescent team sport participants may be related to some social norms around the sport (e.g. the drinking culture associated with amateur rugby union in the United Kingdom).

Variations in coaching approaches may influence socialization and developmental outcomes realized through sport (Fine 1987). However, it is likely that positive and negative outcomes are influenced by complex processes that must take into account broader social and cultural influences (McCormack and Chalip 1988). As Thorlindsson commented many years ago, researchers must ask 'what are the crucial elements in this process?' (1989: 142). Researchers have yet to provide sufficient evidence to answer this question. Such evidence is a primary requirement if sport is to have a direct and sustained impact on youth development.

## Issues for future consideration

One limitation of sport PYD research conducted to date is that all types of sports have been treated together, and researchers have yet to establish if different sporting contexts are associated with different types of developmental experiences. For example, Hansen *et al.* (2003) speculated that negative outcomes arising from sport are due to the unique demands of competition. Although it has been acknowledged that researchers need to examine how competition influences adolescents' social and emotional functioning (Lowe Vandell *et al.* 2005), we were unable to locate any published research which has specifically examined PYD experiences in competitive versus recreational sport contexts. In a similar vein, Pedersen and Seidman (2004) suggested that team sports may provide more opportunities for PYD than individual sports because the team setting is associated with increased social interactions. Again, no published research to date has examined PYD experiences in team versus individual sport contexts. Thus, an important future research direction is to establish what types of developmental experience are associated with distinctly different sporting contexts. For example, participation in competitive versus recreational sport or team versus individual sport may be associated with different types of developmental experience.

Moving beyond contextual issues (i.e. competitive versus recreational contexts, team versus individual contexts), another limitation is that researchers have tended to treat sport as a homogeneous experience for all participants in a particular context. However, sporting experiences may vary across the same type of contexts. Consider the hypothetical example of a coach of a competitive under-16 soccer team who insists that his athletes volunteer as coaches for junior teams, spend time working on charitable endeavors, and demands that the players show respect for each other, the opposition, and the referee. Compare this team environment to that created by the (hypothetical) coach of a rival team who does not embrace any of these values, and rather insists that his players are aggressive, confrontational, and challenge every refereeing decision. It is quite likely that the players on these two teams would encounter very different types of developmental experiences, even though these two teams represent ostensibly similar contexts (i.e. competitive team sport).

To understand how sport is experienced by youth it is important to assess and examine the structure of their sport environment (Mahoney and Stattin 2000). Furthermore, in Chapter 1 of this book, Nicole Zarrett and her colleagues highlighted the importance of considering the intensity and continuity of sports involvement in assessing PYD. To date, researchers have rarely examined these issues. For example, Perkins et al. (2004) conducted a longitudinal study to examine the impact of youth sport participation on engagement in sports and physical fitness activities during young adulthood. Youth sport involvement was measured using items such as 'About how many hours do you usually spend each week taking part in organized sport?' This question provides data about the extent of sport involvement (i.e. number of hours) but it provides no information about the structure of sport and the quality of the respondents' sport experiences. Recognizing this limitation of their study, Perkins et al. concluded that 'future research is needed to identify characteristics of quality sport experiences' (p. 517).

A good example of how to assess the quality of sport experiences was provided by Boone and Leadbeater (2006), who examined the hypothesis that positive team sports involvement mediates the risk of depression among 449 Canadian students from grades 8 to 10. In addition to assessing total amount of team sports involvement, the authors also measured 'positive team sports involvement' using a 16-item questionnaire that asked participants to rate how often positive and negative experiences occur when they are playing team sports. The measure contained three dimensions (with internal consistencies ranging from .74 to .87) that reflected competence (in terms of skill development), positive coaching, and feelings of social support. In addition to using questionnaires, the quality of adolescents' sporting experiences may also be addressed using qualitative techniques to generate alternative, in-depth accounts that can supplement existing quantitative research.

Another factor which we urge researchers and practitioners to consider in developing sport interventions to promote PYD is the effect of peer group interaction. Based on two experimentally controlled intervention studies, Dishion et al. (1999) showed that peer-group interventions for high-risk youth actually *increased* problem behavior and negative life outcomes in adulthood compared with control youth. These findings suggested that, compared to low-risk youth, high-risk youth were particularly vulnerable to peer groupings. Essentially, high-risk youth may learn certain negative behaviors from each other in poorly structured settings. Thus, grouping of high-risk youth can inadvertently reinforce problem behavior. Those interested in creating peer group sport interventions for high-risk youth should be mindful of these findings and ensure that appropriate supervision is provided and programs embrace principles of PYD.

## Summary

It is clear that mere participation does not automatically produce positive development outcomes; rather, positive development will depend on how programs are delivered and experienced and how the sport organization facilitates positive social norms (Petitpas *et al.* 2005). We do believe that sport programs can help to promote positive development among youth. In particular, sport may be an excellent context for teaching youth to develop initiative, regulate emotion, and learn to work as a team. However, to promote other positive outcomes sport leaders will have to embrace specific goals and techniques.

Some caveats should be considered when evaluating the evidence for the benefits of sport participation. Most studies have been correlational, which means that causality cannot be demonstrated. In other words, sport may not produce positive outcomes; positive outcomes may be reported because youth in sport are already well-adjusted prior to their sport participation. The point here is that sport participants may be a self-selected sample. That is, those young athletes who become involved in sport, and stay involved over time, may do so because their values (and their parents' values) are consistent with the type of experiences that sport provides.

We envisage that the future of sport PYD research may involve a melding of principles and practices developed through instructional sport PYD programs into everyday organized sport. We imagine a future where all sport leagues, clubs, and teams have stated goals which are congruent with the objectives of PYD. Administrators, coaches, parents, and athletes will work toward obtaining these objectives while enjoying the physical activity experiences that sport offers. We hope that the suggestions provided in this book stimulate discussion about the best ways to integrate PYD into existing organized sport programs.

## Acknowledgements

In preparing this chapter, Nick Holt was supported by an operating grant from the Social Sciences and Humanities Research Council of Canada, and a Population Health Investigator Award from Alberta Heritage Foundation for Medical Research. These sources of funding are greatly appreciated. We are also grateful to Dr Clare Stevinson for her insightful comments on a previous draft of this chapter.

## References

Akiva, T. (2005) 'Turning training into results: the new youth program quality assessment', *High/Scope Resource*, 24: 21–4.

Audrain-McGovern, J. A., Rodriguez, D., Wileyto, E. P., Schimtz, K. H., and Shields, P. G. (2006) 'Effect of team sport participation on genetic predisposition to adolescent smoking progression', *Archives of General Psychiatry*, 63: 433–41.

Baumert, P. W., Henderson, J. M., and Thompson, N. J. (1998) 'Health risk behaviors of adolescent participants in organized sports', *Journal of Adolescent Health*, 22: 460–5.

Begg, D. J., Langley, J. D., Moffitt, T., and Marshall, S. W. (1996) 'Sport and delinquency: an examination of the deterrence hypothesis in a longitudinal study', *British Journal of Sports Medicine*, 30: 335–41.

Boone, E. M., and Leadbeater, B. J. (2006) 'Game on: diminishing risks for depressive symptoms in early adolescence through positive involvement in team sports', *Journal of Research on Adolescence*, 16: 79–90.

Catalano, R. F., Berglund, M. L., Ryan, J. A. M., Lonczak, H. S., and Hawkins, J. D. (1999) *Positive Youth Development in the United States: Research Findings on Evaluations of Youth Development Programs.* Washington, DC: Department of Health and Human Services.

Davis, T. C., Arnold, C., Nandy, I., Bocchini, J. A., Gottlieb, A., George, R. B., and Berkel, H. (1997) 'Tobacco use among male high school athletes', *Journal of Adolescent Health*, 21: 97–101.

Dishion, T. J., McCord, J., and Poulin, F. (1999) 'When interventions harm: peer groups and problem behavior', *American Psychologist*, 54: 755–64.

Donato, F., Assanelli, D., Chiesa, R., Poeta, M. L., Tomasoni, V., and Turla, C. (1997) 'Cigarette smoking and sports participation in adolescents: a cross-sectional survey among high school students in Italy', *Substance Use and Misuse*, 32: 1555–72.

Dworkin, J. B., Larson, R. W., and Hansen, D. (2003) 'Adolescents' accounts of growth experiences in youth activities', *Journal of Youth and Adolescence*, 32: 17–26.

Eccles, J. S., and Barber, B. L. (1999) 'Student council, volunteering, basketball, or marching band: what kind of extracurricular involvement matters?', *Journal of Adolescent Research*, 14: 10–43.

Eccles, J. S., Barber, B. L., Stone, M., and Hunt, J. (2003) 'Extracurricular activities and adolescent development', *Journal of Social Issues*, 59: 865–89.

Esch, T., and Stefano, G. B. (2004) 'The neurobiology of pleasure, reward processes, addiction and their health implications', *Neuroendocrinological Letters*, 24: 235–42.

Fine, G. A. (1987) *With the Boys: Little League Baseball and Preadolescent Culture.* Chicago: University of Chicago Press.

Garry, J. P., and Morrissey, S. L. (2000) 'Team sports participation and risk-taking behaviors among a biracial middle school population', *Clinical Journal of Sports Medicine*, 10: 185–90.

Greenwald, P., and Cullen, J. (1985) 'The new emphasis in cancer control', *Journal of the National Cancer Institute*, 74: 543–51.

Hansen, D. M., Larson, R. W., and Dworkin, J. B. (2003) 'What adolescents learn in organized youth activities: a survey of self-reported developmental experiences', *Journal of Research on Adolescence*, 13: 25–55.

Holt, N. L. (2007) 'An ethnographic study of positive youth development on a high school soccer team', paper presented at Society for Research in Child Development conference, Boston, MA.

Holt, N. L., and Dunn, J. G. H. (2004) 'Toward a grounded theory of the psychosocial competencies and environmental conditions associated with soccer success', *Journal of Applied Sport Psychology*, 16: 199–219.

Holt, N. L., and Sparkes, A. C. (2001) 'An ethnographic study of cohesiveness on a college soccer team over a season', *The Sport Psychologist*, 15: 237–59.

Holt, N. L., Black, D. E., and Tink, L. (2006) 'Do athletes learn life skills through sport?', paper presented at Association for the Advancement of Applied Sport Psychology Conference, Miami, FL.

Kulig, K., Brener, N. D., and McManus, T. (2003) 'Sexual activity and substance use among adolescents by category of physical activity plus team sports participation', *Archives of Pediatric Adolescence Medicine*, 157: 905–12.

Larson, R. W., Hansen, D. M., and Moneta, G. (2006) 'Differing profiles of developmental experiences across types of organized youth activities', *Developmental Psychology*, 42: 849–63.

Lerner, R. M., Lerner, J. V., Almerigi, J. B., Theokas, C., Phelps, E., Naudeau, S., *et al.* (2005) 'Positive youth development, participation in community youth development programs, and community contributions of fifth-grade adolescents: findings from the first wave of the 4-H study of positive youth development', *Journal of Early Adolescence*, 25: 17–71.

Lorente, F. O., Souville, M., Griffet, J., and Grelot, L. (2004) 'Participation in sports and alcohol consumption among French adolescents', *Addictive Behaviours*, 29: 941–6.

Lowe Vandell, D. L., Pierce, K. M., and Dadisman, K. (2005) 'Out-of-school settings as a developmental context for children and youth', *Advances in Child Development and Behavior*, 33: 43–77.

McCormack, J. B., and Chalip, L. (1988) 'Sport as socialization: a critique of methodological premises', *Social Science Journal*, 25: 83–92.

Mahoney, J. L., and Stattin, H. (2000) 'Leisure activities and adolescent antisocial behaviour: the role of structure and context', *Journal of Adolescence*, 23: 113–27.

Marsh, H. W., and Kleitman, S. (2003) 'School athletic participation: mostly gain with little pain', *Journal of Sport and Exercise Psychology*, 25: 205–28.

Melnick, M. J., Miller, K. E., Sabo, D. F., Farrell, M. P., and Barnes, G. M. (2001) 'Tobacco use among high school athletes and non-athletes: results of the 1997 Youth Risk Behavior Study', *Adolescence*, 36: 727–47.

Miller, K. E., Barnes, G. M, Melnick, M. J., Sabo, D. F., and Farrell, M. P. (2002) 'Gender and racial/ethnic differences in predicting adolescent sexual risk: athletic participation versus exercise', *Journal of Health and Social Behavior*, 43: 436–50.

Morris, L., Sallybanks, J., Willis, K., and Makkai, T. (2003) *Sport, Physical Activity, and Antisocial Behavior in Youth: Trends and Issues in Crime and Criminal Justice.* Canberra: Australian Institute of Criminology.

National Research Council and Institute of Medicine (2002) *Community Programs to Promote Youth Development.* Washington, DC: National Academy Press.

Nicholls, A. R., Holt, N. L., and Polman, R. J. C. (2005) 'A phenomenological analysis of coping effectiveness in golf', *The Sport Psychologist*, 19: 111–30.

Papacharisis, V., Goudas, M., Danish, S. J., and Theodorakis, Y. (2004) 'The effectiveness of teaching a life skills program in a school-based sport context', *Journal of Applied Sport Psychology*, 17: 247–54.

Pate, R. R., Trost, S. G., Levin, S., and Dowda, M. (2000) 'Sports participation and health-related behaviors among US youth', *Archives of Pediatrics and Adolescent Medicine*, 154: 904–11.

Pederson, S., and Seidman, E. (2004) 'Team sports achievement and self-esteem development among urban adolescent girls', *Psychology of Women Quarterly*, 28: 412–22.

Peretti-Watel, P., Beck, F., and Legleye, S. (2002) 'Beyond the U-curve: the relationship between sport and alcohol, cigarette and cannabis use in adolescents', *Addiction*, 97: 707–16.

Peretti-Watel, P., Guagliardo, V., Verger, P., Pruvost, J., Mignon, P., and Obadia, Y. (2003) 'Sporting activity and drug use: alcohol, cigarette and cannabis use among elite student athletes', *Addiction*, 98: 1249–56.

Perkins, D. F., Jacobs, J. E., Barber, B. L., and Eccles, J. S. (2004) 'Childhood and adolescent sports participation as predictors of participation in sports and physical fitness activities during young adulthood', *Youth and Society*, 35: 495–520.

Petitpas, A. J., Cornelius, A. E., Van Raalte, J. L., and Jones, T. (2005) 'A framework for planning youth sport programs that foster psychosocial development', *The Sport Psychologist*, 19: 63–80.

Petlichkoff, L. M. (1996) 'The drop-out dilemma in youth sports', in O. Bar-Or (ed.), *The Child and Adolescent Athlete*, pp. 418–30. Oxford: Blackwell.

Rainey, C. J., McKeown, R. E., Sargent, R. G., and Valois, R. F. (1996) 'Patterns of tobacco and alcohol use among sedentary, exercising, nonathletic, and athletic youth', *Journal of School Health*, 66: 27–32.

Rodriguez, D., and Audrain-McGovern, J. (2004) 'Team sport participation and smoking: analysis with general growth mixture modeling', *Journal of Pediatric Psychology*, 29: 299–308.

Roth, J., and Brooks-Gunn, J. (2003) 'Youth development programs: risk, prevention, and policy', *Journal of Adolescent Health*, 32: 170–82.

Thorlindsson, T. (1989) 'Sport participation, smoking, and drug and alcohol use among Icelandic youth', *Sociology of Sport Journal*, 6: 136–43.

# Index

eBooks – at www.eBookstore.tandf.co.uk

## A library at your fingertips!

eBooks are electronic versions of printed books. You can store them on your PC/laptop or browse them online.

They have advantages for anyone needing rapid access to a wide variety of published, copyright information.

eBooks can help your research by enabling you to bookmark chapters, annotate text and use instant searches to find specific words or phrases. Several eBook files would fit on even a small laptop or PDA.

**NEW:** Save money by eSubscribing: cheap, online access to any eBook for as long as you need it.

## Annual subscription packages

We now offer special low-cost bulk subscriptions to packages of eBooks in certain subject areas. These are available to libraries or to individuals.

For more information please contact webmaster.ebooks@tandf.co.uk

We're continually developing the eBook concept, so keep up to date by visiting the website.

## www.eBookstore.tandf.co.uk